THE CHILD WITHIN HAS BEEN AWAKENED BUT THE OLD LADY ON THE OUTSIDE JUST COLLAPSED

THE CHILD WITHIN HAS BEEN AWAKENED BUT THE OLD LADY ON THE OUTSIDE JUST COLLAPSED

A *Cathy*® Collection by Cathy Guisewite

Andrews and McMeel
A Universal Press Syndicate Company
Kansas City

5

29-MINUTE PHOTOS... 4-MINUTE DINNERS... INSTANT CASH, CREDIT, PRINTING, SOUP, REPLAYS, CALCULATIONS AND GRATIFICATION...

THE HIGH-POWERED, MEGA-ENERGY, WARP-SPEED '90s WOMAN HURLS TOWARD THE HOLIDAY SEASON WITH A SUPERSONIC NEW CONFIDENCE IN WHAT'S POSSIBLE...

IF I CAN'T FAX MY FAT SOMEWHERE, THEN LET ME SHIP IT OVERNIGHT DELIVERY!!

THROW ANOTHER RICE CAKE DOWN THE HALL. SHE'S CRACKING.

DON'T ASK IF SHE HAS A DATE FOR THANKSGIVING... DON'T ASK IF SHE HAS A DATE FOR THANKSGIVING...

IT'S TOO SOON TO PUSH... IT'S TOO SOON TO PUSH... FOCUS FOCUS FOCUS BREATHE BREATHE BREATHE

DON'T PUSH
DON'T PUSH
DON'T PUSH
DON'T PUSH
DON'T PUSH

HOW OLD MUST MY DAUGHTER BE BEFORE OUR ENCOUNTERS QUIT DUPLICATING THE BIRTH EXPERIENCE?

IF YOU COME FOR THANKSGIVING, MY PARENTS WILL SPEND THE WHOLE TIME SECRETLY ANALYZING YOU AND YOUR POTENTIAL FUTURE WITH ME, IRVING.

IF YOU DON'T COME, THEY'LL SPEND THE NEXT YEAR SPECULATING ON CHARACTER FLAWS THAT WOULD PREVENT YOU FROM WANTING TO ATTEND A FAMILY EVENT.

WOULD YOU RATHER BE SCRUTINIZED IN PERSON, KNOWING THAT EVERY WORD YOU SAY WILL BE REHASHED IN FUTURE FAMILY DISCUSSIONS...OR WOULD YOU RATHER BE PICKED APART IN ABSENTIA, WITH NO HOPE OF DEFENDING YOURSELF?

OOF.

LET THE HAPPY HOLIDAYS BEGIN, MOTHER!

WHEN IRVING SEES MY PICTURE AT CATHY'S HOUSE, IT'S A LITTLE AD FOR HOW CATHY WILL LOOK DOWN THE ROAD...

WHEN IRVING HEARS MY VOICE ON CATHY'S ANSWERING MACHINE, IT'S A LITTLE RADIO SPOT FOR HOW CATHY WILL SOUND IN THE FUTURE...

NOW IRVING'S COMING FOR THANKSGIVING DINNER! UP CLOSE AND IN PERSON! PRIME TIME! WASH THE DRAPES! POLISH THE CHINA! PULL OUT THE GOOD CLOTHES!

TO A FATHER, IT'S A MEAL. TO A MOTHER, IT'S AN INFOMERCIAL.

CALL THE BEAUTY PARLOR! MAKEOVER EMERGENCY!

NO MATTER WHAT HAPPENS AT THANKSGIVING DINNER, I WANT YOU TO KNOW I AM NOT LIKE MY MOTHER, IRVING.

I DON'T THINK LIKE MY MOTHER! I DON'T ACT LIKE MY MOTHER! I AM NOTHING LIKE MY MOTHER!

IRVING! COME HERE, YOU BIG, STRONG HANDSOME MAN! LET ME FLUFF UP SOME PILLOWS, GET YOU A NICE, WARM DRINK AND PLAY A TAPE OF FOOTBALL HIGHLIGHTS FOR YOU WHILE I FINISH COOKING YOUR FIVE-COURSE FEAST!

WHY AREN'T YOU MORE LIKE YOUR MOTHER?

WHERE'S IRVING, DAD?

THE KITCHEN. I THINK MOM'S GIVING HIM THE PIE TREATMENT.

THE PIE TREATMENT?? WHERE SHE FEEDS HIM PIE UNTIL HE TALKS?? I HAVE TO RESCUE HIM!! IRVING, I'M COMING!! I'M...

...AND HOW MANY CHILDREN DO YOU THINK YOU MIGHT WANT??

WHERE'S IRVING, CATHY?

WHO AM I TO MESS WITH THE MASTER?

If I wait until the last second to buy gifts, I'll be desperate and will spend twice what I planned.

If I start buying now, I'll find other things I like better later, and will spend twice what I planned.

If I wait until the exact mid-point between too early and too late, I'll panic because the ideal shopping window is so small, and will spend twice what I planned.

All I want for Christmas is to win the lottery.

Where's the sale price?

Shoppers got immune to sales, so we switched to everyday low prices!

Ho, hum.

Deeply discounted, rolled back, everyday low prices!

Nah...

Mercilessly slashed, cost-crushed, bargain bonanza, rock bottom everyday low prices!!!

How's it going?

Our $50,000 of inventory is intact, but we're completely out of adjectives.

What should I wear? What are you going to wear? What do you think everyone else is going to wear?

Should I take someone? Are you taking someone? Should we go together? Should we go together, but take separate cars? What time should we go? Should I bring a gift? Are you bringing a gift? Who's going to be there? What should I wear?

The holiday party: three weeks of mental and physical preparation, culminating in one glorious moment...

How soon can we leave?

JOAN SENT ME A CHRISTMAS CARD LAST YEAR, BUT I DIDN'T SEND HER A CARD. DO I SEND HER A CARD THIS YEAR OR NOT?

BRENDA **DIDN'T** SEND A CARD LAST YEAR, BUT I SENT **HER** A CARD...SO THIS YEAR **SHE** SENT A CARD. DO I SEND HER A CARD OR NOT?

ONLY DEBBIE HAD THE IN-SIGHT TO QUIT SENDING ME A CARD THE EXACT YEAR I QUIT SENDING HER A CARD! SHE READ MY MIND... SHE KNEW ME SO WELL...THE UN-SPOKEN, HARMONIOUS BOND OF A TRUE FRIEND...

...I THINK I'LL SEND HER A CARD.

WHERE'S THE ESCALATOR?? EVERYTHING I NEED IS ON THE SECOND FLOOR! DOES ANY-ONE KNOW WHERE THEY HID THE ESCALATOR??!

I CAN'T FIND THE ESCALATOR! I'M TRAPPED, SPIRALING END-LESSLY IN AN ACRE OF PINE-SCENTED POTPOURRI! I'M CHOKING FOR AIR! I CAN'T BREATHE! GASPING CHOKING SPIRALING I'M GOING TO DIE LOOKING FOR THE ESCALATOR!!

BUT FIRST I NEED A LADIES' ROOM! THE LADIES' ROOM'S ON THREE! WHERE'S THE ESCA-LATOR TO THREE?? I RE-FUSE TO DIE UNTIL I CAN USE THE LADIES' ROOM! CLEAR AWAY THIS YULE-TIDE DEBRIS AND GET ME ON AN ESCALATOR TO THREE!!

I FINISHED ALL MY SHOPPING ON MY LUNCH BREAK.

OH, SHUT UP.

WHEN I WAS YOUNG, I HAD TIME BUT NO MONEY. I GAVE GIFTS THAT WERE LOVINGLY MADE BY MY OWN LITTLE HANDS.

WHEN I WAS OLDER, I HAD MONEY BUT NO TIME. I GAVE GIFTS THAT WERE LOVINGLY MADE BY SOMEONE ELSE'S HANDS.

NOW I'M OLDER. I HAVE NO TIME, NO MONEY, TEN TIMES THE PEOPLE TO SHOP FOR, AND A LIFELONG REPUTATION FOR GIVING UNIQUE, MEANINGFUL, HANDMADE-BY-SOMEONE, PERSONALLY SIGNIFICANT GIFTS.

MAY I HELP YOU?

TURN ME INTO THE SORT OF PERSON WHO COULD GIVE SOMEONE A PRE-WRAPPED APPLIANCE!

TOO MANY DECISIONS...
TOO MANY PROJECTS...
TOO MANY MIRACLES TO
PERFORM IN TOO LITTLE TIME...

TOO MANY OBLIGATIONS...
TOO MANY PEOPLE...
TOO MANY CARS...

THE CONTEMPORARY WOMAN
STAGGERS HOME, CURLS UP
WITH HER LOVED ONE AND
TAKES COMFORT IN ONE SIMPLE
MESSAGE OF HOPE FOR THE
HOLIDAY SEASON...

"ORDER BY NOON ON
DECEMBER 23, AND WE
GUARANTEE DELIVERY
BY CHRISTMAS."

YOUR MOTHER COOKED AND CLEANED ALL WEEK PREPARING FOR YOUR VISIT, CATHY!

YOUR FATHER WAS UP ALL NIGHT FIXING THE BED IN YOUR LITTLE ROOM!

YOUR MOTHER WASHED AND IRONED YOUR LITTLE CURTAINS!

YOUR FATHER GOT OUT ALL YOUR FAVORITE GAMES!

YOUR MOTHER HASN'T SLEPT FOR DAYS, SHE'S SO EXCITED!

YOUR FATHER STOOD AT THE WINDOW FOR FOUR HOURS IN CASE YOU CAME EARLY!

A WOMAN, HER DOG, AND
THEIR LUGGAGE STAND
PARALYZED ON THE
THRESHOLD OF GUILT.

THE HOLIDAY VISIT
PHASE 1:
OUTFITS: STUNNING
ATTITUDE: IMPECCABLE

PARDON ME WHILE I POWDER
MY NOSE BEFORE WE DINE.

PHASE 2:
OUTFITS: CASUAL
ATTITUDE: RELAXED

NO USE IN DIRTYING
THE GOOD NAPKINS.
IT'S JUST FAMILY.

PHASE 3:
OUTFITS: DUMPY
ATTITUDE: PRE-COMATOSE

GRAB ME A PLATE OF THOSE
LEFTOVERS THAT CATHY
FOUND IN THE KITCHEN, DEAR.

PHASE 4:
LOWEST COMMON DENO-
MINATOR IS ACHIEVED.

WHO'S FOR SKIPPING DINNER
AND JUST EATING THE GIFT I
BAKED FOR THE JOHNSTONS?

I'VE BEEN HERE FIVE DAYS, MOM AND DAD. I GIVE IN. I ACCEPT MY STATUS AS A SIX-YEAR-OLD. I'M NOT FIGHTING IT ANYMORE.

FEED ME WHAT YOU WANT! TELL ME I'LL CATCH PNEUMONIA IF I DON'T WEAR SOCKS! PEEK IN MY ROOM TO MAKE SURE I'M NOT STAYING UP PAST MY BEDTIME!

ASK IF I REMEMBERED TO FLOSS! PARADE YOUR FRIENDS' SINGLE SONS IN FRONT OF ME! I GIVE UP! I SUCCUMB! YOU WIN! YOUR TINY HELPLESS BABY IS ALL YOURS AGAIN!!

PARTY POOPER.

18

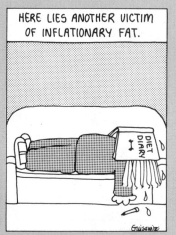

WAITED TEN MINUTES FOR DEFECTIVE ELEVATOR AT OFFICE.

1 2 3 4 5 6 7 8

TAP TAP

CIRCLED LOT FOR TWENTY MINUTES BEFORE PARKING SPOT NEAR MALL ENTRANCE OPENED UP.

HONK HONK

FUMED FOR FIFTEEN MINUTES WHILE MAINTENANCE CREW RESTORED ESCALATOR POWER.

FUME FUME

MALL

Mall Maintenance

DIET SETBACK #4: CAN'T EXERCISE BECAUSE DON'T OWN A STEP.

OPEN UP! MY METABOLISM RATE IS PLUMMETING!!!

CLOSED

SPORTS EQUIPME[N]

HALF AN OLD CHOCOLATE BAR... I MUST HAVE HIDDEN IT IN MY DESK DRAWER MONTHS AGO...

I REMEMBER WHEN I DIDN'T HAVE TO HIDE CHOCOLATE... DAD USED TO BUY ME CHOCOLATE ON SATURDAY... CHOCOLATE USED TO MAKE ME HAPPY, NOT GUILTY...

CATHY

... WELL, WE FELT A LITTLE GUILTY BECAUSE MOM DIDN'T KNOW... BUT IT WAS HAPPY GUILTY, NOT GUILTY GUILTY. IT WAS TEAMWORK GUILT. A SPECIAL FATHER-DAUGHTER WEEKEND GUILT CELEBRATION...

DIET SETBACK #5: WAVE OF NOSTALGIA WASHED OVER BRAIN, SUCKED WILLPOWER OUT TO SEA AND HALF A STALE CANDY BAR DOWN THROAT.

...MY DIET? I'M DOING GREAT ON MY DIET, MOM!

HOW BADLY HAVE YOU BLOWN IT, DEAR?

I HAVEN'T BLOWN IT!

YOU'RE TOO CHEERFUL TO HAVE NOT BLOWN IT!

CAN'T I SOUND CHEERFUL BECAUSE I'M DOING WELL??

YOU COULD, EXCEPT YOU'RE RELATED TO ME. I HEAR BAKED GOODS IN YOUR VOICE, JUST AS MY MOTHER COULD HEAR THEM IN MY VOICE, AND HER MOTHER COULD HEAR THEM IN HERS.

DIET SETBACK #6-#6000: GENETICS.

ONE TINY PIECE OF PIE, OK??!

OOPS!... AND I DETECT A BAG OF SOMETHING SALTY IN THE VERY NEAR FUTURE...

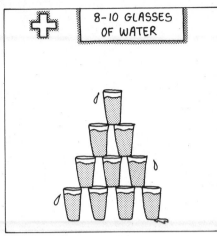

IN 1970, WE FOUGHT EVERY INJUSTICE... TODAY, I DON'T HAVE TIME TO RETURN ONE DEFECTIVE APPLIANCE.

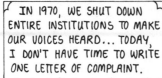

IN 1970, WE SHUT DOWN ENTIRE INSTITUTIONS TO MAKE OUR VOICES HEARD... TODAY, I DON'T HAVE TIME TO WRITE ONE LETTER OF COMPLAINT.

IN 1970, WE ORGANIZED A GENERATION TO REVOLUTIONIZE THE PRIORITIES AND POLITICS OF THE WHOLE SOCIAL STRUCTURE... TODAY, I DON'T HAVE THE ENERGY TO LOOK UP ONE PHONE NUMBER AND MENTION I'M DISSATISFIED.

REBEL WITHOUT A COFFEEMAKER.

AN ORGANIZED HOME IS A TRANQUIL HOME!

MOTHER...

A TRANQUIL HOME IS AN INVITING HOME!

AN INVITING HOME IS ONE IN WHICH LOVE CAN IGNITE INTO A BURNING PASSION THAT COULD PROPEL YOU INTO MARRIAGE, BABIES AND A LIFETIME OF HAPPINESS!

AT LAST. I'VE SEEN THE WAY TO THE ALTAR, AND IT'S LINED WITH SHELF PAPER.

SNIP SNIP

WHY ARE YOU REALLY HERE, MOTHER?

BECAUSE THERE'S STILL TIME FOR YOU, CATHY!

YOU ONLY HAVE 20 YEARS OF PHOTOS STUFFED IN SHOE BOXES, NOT 60... YOU ONLY HAVE FIVE YEARS OF UNFILED RECEIPTS AND UNMENDED CLOTHES, NOT 45... YOU ONLY HAVE THREE OVERFLOWING JUNK DRAWERS...

PLEASE! LET ME LIVE THROUGH YOU! LET ME HELP YOU ACHIEVE THE GOAL I COULD SEE, BUT NEVER QUITE GRASP!

SOME MOTHERS DREAM OF FAME AND FORTUNE. MINE DREAMS OF A CUPBOARD THAT WILL SHUT.

I DEDICATE THIS CARAMEL TO IRVING, WHO SPENT SIX MONTHS PREPARING TO WATCH THE SUPERBOWL, BUT WHO THINKS VALENTINE'S DAY IS JUST "MEDIA HYPE"!

I DEDICATE THESE PEANUT BUTTER CLUSTERS TO JAKE, JIM AND TOM, WHO "WEREN'T READY FOR COMMITMENT" AND THEN MARRIED SOMEONE ELSE!

I DEDICATE ALL THE DISGUSTING CHOCOLATE CREMES TO BOBBY, RICK, DAVE AND BILLY, WHO IGNORED ME IN THE THIRD GRADE AND BEGAN A CYCLE OF INSECURITY WHICH HAS HELPED TRASH EVERY RELATIONSHIP SINCE!

ONCE AGAIN, CUPID HAS LIFTED HIS LITTLE BOW AND SHOT ME IN THE STOMACH.

TELL ME WHAT IT'S LIKE TO BE MARRIED, MARGO.

IT'S EXACTLY LIKE DATING, EXCEPT YOU SEE EACH OTHER AT YOUR ABSOLUTE WORST AND HE NEVER GOES HOME.

TELL ME WHAT IT'S LIKE TO BE MARRIED, KAREN.

IT'S A 24-HOUR-A-DAY, 365-DAY-A-YEAR JOB OF COMPROMISE, COMPROMISE, COMPROMISE!

TELL ME WHAT IT'S LIKE TO BE MARRIED, CATHY.

IT'S A BLISSFUL UNION OF TWO SOULS, INTER-TWINED IN UN-ENDING PASSION AND JOY!!!

FUNNY HOW YOU ONLY GET THE TRUTH WHEN YOU ASK SOMEONE WHO HASN'T BEEN THERE.

WHAT IRKS ME IS THAT THIS WHOLE CHAOTIC PRE-WEDDING YEAR DOESN'T REALLY "COUNT" AS A YEAR OF BEING TOGETHER WITH SIMON, CATHY.

WHY IS THE STRENGTH OF RELATIONSHIPS ONLY MEAS-URED BY YEARS OF MARRIAGE, WHEN THE REAL TEST IS IN THOSE HIDEOUS, FRAGILE MONTHS WHEN YOU'RE TECHNICALLY EN-GAGED, BUT ARE BOTH FREE TO WALK, AND DON'T??

I DEMAND RELATION-SHIP CREDIT FOR MY ENGAGE-MENT YEAR!

THEN I SHOULD GET A LIFETIME-ACHIEVEMENT AWARD FOR ALL MY YEARS WITH IRVING!

NONSENSE. YOU'RE ONLY DATING. EACH YEAR TOGETHER WITHOUT A PROPOSAL COUNTS AS A DEMERIT.

WHEN YOU STORMED IN HERE A YEAR AGO, I TOLD YOU INVITATIONS COULDN'T BE ENGRAVED IN A WEEK.

WHEN YOU STOMPED BACK IN NINE, SIX, THREE AND TWO MONTHS AGO, I TOLD YOU INVITATIONS COULDN'T BE ENGRAVED IN A WEEK.

THAT'S CORRECT! AND IF YOU DON'T TELL ME YOU CAN ENGRAVE INVITATIONS IN A WEEK TODAY, I'LL BE COMING BACK HOURLY TO WHIMPER, WHINE AND GROVEL!

OH, FOR CRYING OUT LOUD. I'LL SEE WHAT I CAN DO.

THERE'S NOTHING A STORE LOVES LIKE HAVING YOU USE UP YOUR AGGRAVATION CREDIT LINE.

Panel 1: JUST BECAUSE MOMMY'S AT HOME ALL DAY DOESN'T MEAN MOMMY'S PLACE IS **ONLY** IN THE HOME, GUS.

Panel 2: LOTS OF MOMMIES GO TO AN OFFICE WHILE THE DADDIES STAY HOME. DADDIES CAN STAY HOME JUST LIKE MOMMIES! MOMMIES CAN GO TO AN OFFICE JUST LIKE DADDIES! IT'S EXACTLY THE SAME! SO WHEN **YOU** GROW UP...

Panel 3: DADDY LOST HIS JOB TODAY. MOMMY BETTER START LOOKING.

Panel 4: AAUGH!

MOMMY HAS A PIECE OF RHETORIC STUCK IN HER THROAT.

Panel 5: ONE DAY I HAVE A BRILLIANT CAREER AND THE NEXT DAY MY JOB IS ELIMINATED! **HOW COULD THEY DO THIS TO ME, ANDREA?!**

Panel 6: OH LUKE...THEY DIDN'T DO IT TO YOU. THE WHOLE COUNTRY'S HURTING. LOTS OF GREAT PEOPLE ARE OUT OF WORK.

Panel 7: YOU CAN'T TAKE IT PERSONALLY. IT ISN'T ABOUT YOU. IT'S ABOUT ALL OF US. WE'RE ALL IN IT TOGETHER, AND I'M IN IT WITH YOU.

Panel 8: I KNOW. YOU'LL HAVE TO SUPPORT US FOR A WHILE.

HOW COULD THEY DO THIS TO ME??!

Panel 9: LET'S NOT PANIC, LUKE. WE CAN LIVE OFF OUR SAVINGS WHILE YOU LOOK FOR ANOTHER JOB.

Panel 10: WE SPENT PART OF OUR SAVINGS DOING THE BABY'S ROOM IN KNOTTY PINE TO REFLECT OUR "RETURN TO SIMPLER TIMES"... ...WE SPENT PART REPLACING OUR HIGH-TECH KITCHEN WITH DISTRESSED OAK TO SYMBOLIZE OUR REPULSION WITH CONSPICUOUS CONSUMPTION...

Panel 11: AND WE SPENT THE REST ON THE NATURAL FIBER AREA RUG -- WHICH IS ROLLED UP IN THE BASEMENT SO NO ONE GETS IT DIRTY -- TO VOICE OUR ONENESS WITH THE EARTH.

Panel 12: WE HAVE NOTHING TO FALL BACK ON??

JUST THE $500 HAND-LOOMED, THIRD-WORLD THROW PILLOWS ON THE ADIRONDACK ROCKER.

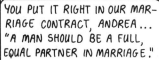

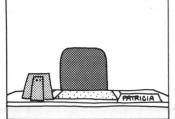

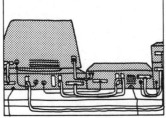

HOW ARE WE DOING, CATHY? ... TEMP NUMBER ONE SENT NINE CLIENTS INTO PHONE ORBIT BEFORE RIPPING THE CORD OUT OF THE WALL.

TEMP NUMBER TWO RAN OUT SHRIEKING THAT SHE WAS DRAGGING MARGO FROM HER SICK BED IF SHE DIDN'T TELL WHERE SHE HID THE COMMAND SEQUENCE TO OPEN THE FILES.

TEMP NUMBER THREE SNAPPED, SENT LEWD NOTES THROUGH E-MAIL, AND THEN ATTEMPTED TO FAX A BEAN BURRITO TO THE AGENCY THAT SENT HER.

WELL, I'M SURE NUMBER FOUR WILL BE THE CHARM! ... NUMBER FOUR IS IN THE LADIES ROOM GIVING A SWIRLEY TO THE COPIER REPAIRMAN.

I WORKED LATE EVERY NIGHT THIS WEEK. I AM NOT GOING TO WORK ALL WEEKEND!

I'M NOT GOING TO DO IT! I HAVE A LIFE! I DESERVE A LIFE! I AM GOING TO LIVE MY LIFE!

WORKAHOLIC: TWIN SISTER OF THE AVOID-AHOLIC.

EVERYONE'S STILL OUT SICK?? ... MARGO ISN'T TECHNICALLY STILL SICK, BUT SINCE SHE WAS SICK LAST WEEK, SHE FELT SHE DESERVED A "PITY DAY."

TIM, WHO WAS SICK ON SATURDAY AND SUNDAY, IS TAKING AN "I GOT CHEATED OUT OF MY WEEKEND" DAY.

GEORGE, WHO HAD TO COVER FOR MARGO AND TIM ALL WEEK, IS TAKING A "REVENGE DAY"... AND JOAN, WHO THINKS EVERYONE'S BEEN FAKING IT ALL ALONG, IS TAKING A "ME TOO" DAY.

FORGET THE ANTIBIOTICS. WHAT THIS OFFICE NEEDS ARE SOME ANTI-NEUROTICS.

Panel 1: AFTER NINE FAILED TRIES, THE TEMP AGENCY IS SENDING OVER A WOMAN WITH A MASTER'S DEGREE IN COMPUTER SCIENCE.

Panel 2: SHE HEADED A TEN-PERSON SYSTEMS ANALYST DEPARTMENT IN HER LAST JOB...

Panel 3: ...AND HAS BEEN DOING FREE-LANCE DATABASE CONSULTING FROM HER HOME SINCE THE BIRTH OF HER SECOND CHILD. IN SHORT, MR. PINKLEY, SHE'S...

Panel 4: OVERQUALIFIED FOR ANY-THING BUT $6.50 PER HOUR CLERICAL TEMP WORK!

ANDREA...YOU??

SHOULD HAVE HELD OUT FOR $5.25, SHE LOOKS DESPERATE.

Panel 5: I WAS EARNING $60,000 A YEAR WHEN I QUIT WORKING FULL TIME TO BE A MOTHER... ...AND NOW ALL I'M WORTH IS A $6.50-AN-HOUR TEMP JOB??

Panel 6: DO PEOPLE THINK I'M NOT SERIOUS ABOUT MY CAREER JUST BECAUSE I HAVE CHIL-DREN??...THAT I'M INCAPABLE OF THE KIND OF FOCUS THAT GOT ME TO THE TOP BEFORE??

Panel 7: IT'S AN OUTRAGE I INTEND TO FIGHT, BUT FOR NOW THERE'S WORK TO DO! WHERE SHALL I GET STARTED ON THOSE?

Panel 8: THERE'S AN INCH OF SPACE BETWEEN GUS' FIRST BATH PHOTO AND ZENITH'S BIRTH-DAY ALBUM.

THIS IS MY DESK?? YOU'RE KID-DING. I THOUGHT IT WAS AN END TABLE.

Panel 9: ...AND THEN THE COMPANY SHOULD...WHAT WAS THAT??

WHAT? WHAT WAS WHAT??

Panel 10: I HAD AN UNINTERRUPTED THOUGHT! AN UNINTER-RUPTED THOUGHT FORMED IN MY HEAD AND ACTUALLY MADE IT OUT OF MY MOUTH!

Panel 11: I HAD MY FIRST UNINTER-RUPTED THOUGHT SINCE I QUIT WORKING FULL TIME TO BE WITH THE CHILDREN!!!

Panel 12: ...THE CHILDREN! I HAVE TO CALL HOME! GUS IS DUE FOR A BOTTLE AND IT'S ZENITH'S STORY HOUR!!

ANOTHER MOTHER BEGINS AND ENDS QUALITY TIME WITH HER BRAIN.

A PILE OF OVERDUE CORRESPONDENCE... ANDREA, OUR TEMP, HAD IT ANSWERED IN THE EQUIVALENT OF HER DAUGHTER'S NAPTIME.

FILES HOPELESSLY HEAPED IN THE CONFERENCE ROOM ... ANDREA, OUR TEMP, HAD THEM ORGANIZED IN THE EQUIVALENT OF HER SON'S "BARNEY" VIDEO.

IN ONE WEEK, ANDREA HAS ACCOMPLISHED MORE THAN TEN OF US BUMBLING AROUND FOR A MONTH!

...WELL. **THAT** WAS NAUSEATING.

LEAVE IT TO A MOTHER TO INSPIRE US TO NEW DEPTHS.

ANDREA CAME TO WORK AS A CLERICAL TEMP IN MY OFFICE THIS WEEK, MOM. HER HUSBAND LOST HIS JOB, SHE CAN'T FIND ONE, AND THEY HAVE TWO KIDS TO SUPPORT...

ON ONE HAND, IT'S GREAT TO SEE AN OLD FRIEND, BUT I HAVE SO MANY CONFLICTING FEELINGS... SHE'S ALWAYS HAD A WAY OF INTIMIDATING ME AND MAKING ME FEEL SO INADEQUATE...

MY CAREER WAS THE ONE PART OF MY LIFE SHE COULDN'T COMMENT ON BECAUSE SHE'D NEVER BEEN THERE IN PERSON... OH, I DON'T KNOW, MOM... IT'S JUST BEEN KIND OF HARD...

WHAT'S NEW WITH CATHY?

SHE TALKED TO SOMEONE WITH A BABY THIS WEEK!

YOUR WEDDING INVITATION WILL SET THE TONE FOR THE WHOLE WEDDING, CHARLENE.

← ENGRAVING →

IT'S YOUR DAY... YOUR MOMENT ... THE SPECIAL WORDS YOU CHOOSE SHOULD CONVEY THE UNIQUE AND PROFOUND EMOTION YOU BRING TO THIS MOST GLORIOUS EVENT!

U.S. MAIL

Nyeh nyeh nyeh nyeh nyeh

I UNDERSTAND WHY YOU KEPT YOUR DISTANCE FROM ME THIS WEEK, IRVING...

THERE'S SO MUCH EMOTIONAL TENSION AROUND AN EVENT LIKE THIS... NO ONE'S LIFE CHANGES WITHOUT ALL OF OUR LIVES CHANGING.

CHARLENE AND SIMON'S WEDDING WILL HAVE A PROFOUND IMPACT ON ALL OF US!

THAT'S THIS WEEKEND? YOU'RE KIDDING.

IF MEN'S HAIR FALLS OUT, IT'S BECAUSE THERE'S NOTHING IN THERE FOR IT TO HOLD ONTO.

WE'VE CHANGED THE DATE TEN TIMES, SPANNING FOUR SEASONS AND SIX DECORATING TRENDS, SWEETHEART...

WE'VE CHANGED THE GUEST LIST 35 TIMES, CAUSING RIPPLE EFFECT CHANGES IN THE CATERING, ENTERTAINMENT, CENTERPIECES AND SEATING ARRANGEMENTS...

...AND NOW, WITH NINE DAYS TO GO, YOUR MOTHER WANTS ME TO CHANGE THE COLOR SCHEME TO MATCH THE MOTHER-OF-THE-GROOM DRESS SHE JUST FOUND ??!

SHE'S ON HER FIRST MARRIAGE AND HER EIGHTY-THIRD WEDDING.

...OH, NO. YOU HAVE THAT "MY GIRLFRIEND'S GETTING MARRIED" LOOK!

...NO! WAIT! IT'S THE "ALL MY FRIENDS HAVE BABIES" LOOK!

...NO! WAIT! ONE EYE IS THE "MY GIRLFRIEND'S GETTING MARRIED" LOOK, AND THE OTHER EYE IS THE "ALL MY FRIENDS HAVE BABIES" LOOK!

AAACK!!

...Tonight I drove him wild with a single glance...

MY WEDDING'S IN SIX DAYS! IN SIX DAYS I'M ESCAPING THE DOOM OF SINGLENESS AND BECOMING A BRIDE!!

EVEN IF THE MARRIAGE FAILS, I WILL HAVE DONE IT! I GET TO CHECK IT OFF THE LIST!

I WILL NEVER HAVE TO GO BACK TO THE WRETCHED STATUS OF THE "NEVER MARRIED WOMAN"! NOT ONE MORE MOMENT IN THAT ROTTING, BITTER WASTELAND!! THE DECK OF LIFE HAS BEEN RESHUFFLED, AND I AM NEVER GOING TO BE THE "OLD MAID"!!!

BUT DON'T WORRY, CATHY. WE'LL STILL BE FRIENDS.

OH, BOY.

Panel 1: THE RENTAL SHOP PULLED OUT SOME OTHER SIZES OF MAID-OF-HONOR DRESSES IN CASE THAT'S TOO...

NO! IT FITS! HA, HA! OF COURSE IT FITS! IT'S A...

Panel 2:

...AACK! THIS IS A SIZE 12! I'M NOT GOING TO BE A SIZE 12 FOR YOUR WEDDING!

THE WEDDING'S IN FIVE DAYS, CATHY. WE'LL TAKE THE SIZE 12.

Panel 3:

I HAVE FIVE DAYS! AFTER ALL THESE YEARS, YOU KNOW THE KIND OF TRANSFORMATION I CAN MAKE IN FIVE DAYS!!!

Panel 4:

WE'LL TAKE THE SIZE 12, BUT PUT A HOLD ON THE SIZE 14.

Gown Rentals

Panel 5:

I RENTED THE TUXES, THE BRIDE GOWN, THE BRIDESMAID DRESSES, THE HALL, THE TABLES, THE CHAIRS, THE CHINA, THE LINENS, THE CENTERPIECES, THE PHONEY ORCHIDS, THE PLASTIC GLASSES AND THE FAKE LACE.

Panel 6:

AFTER THE WEDDING, EVERY SINGLE THING WILL BE THROWN OUT, EATEN OR RETURNED.

Panel 7:

MONTHS OF WORK, AND ALL I'M GOING TO HAVE TO SHOW FOR IT IS A HUSBAND!!

Panel 8:

THERE WENT THE BRIDE.

HERE COMES THE THERAPIST.

Panel 9:

IF I'D GOTTEN MARRIED FIFTEEN YEARS AGO, MY MOTHER WOULD HAVE TAKEN CHARGE OF THE WHOLE EVENT...

Panel 10:

IF I'D GOTTEN MARRIED TEN YEARS AGO, SHE WOULD HAVE LOVINGLY PORED OVER EVERY DETAIL...

Panel 11:

AS IT IS, MY MOTHER'S ENTIRE CONTRIBUTION TO THE WEDDING HAS BEEN TO RUN UP AND DOWN THE MALL SHRIEKING AT THE TOP OF HER LUNGS THAT I'M FINALLY GETTING MARRIED.

Panel 12:

OH, FOR CRYING OUT LOUD. I'LL GET MY MOM TO HELP.

YOUR MOM'S RUNNING AFTER HER HANDING OUT FLIERS THAT SAY YOU'RE STILL AVAILABLE.

GOOD LUCK TOMORROW, SWEETIE!

TRANSLATION: "YOUR LAST SINGLE GIRLFRIEND IS MARRYING A MAN YOU REJECTED FOR NOTHING."

YOU'LL LOOK SO PRETTY!

"200 PEOPLE WHO COULD HAVE BEEN YOUR IN-LAWS WILL BE WATCHING YOU TRUNDLE DOWN THE AISLE IN A SIZE 14 MAID-OF-HONOR DRESS."

WE LOVE YOU! GET A GOOD NIGHT'S SLEEP!

"THIS WOULD BE AN EXTREMELY BAD TIME FOR THAT INSOMNIA-INDUCED SKIN PROBLEM YOU GET TO KICK IN."

AFTER ALL THESE YEARS, THERE'S STILL NOTHING THAT ROCKS ME LIKE MY MOTHER'S LULLABYE.

WHEN I WAS FIVE, I USED TO PLAY WITH MY BRIDE DOLL AND DREAM OF THE DAY I'D MARCH DOWN THE AISLE AND EVERYONE WOULD LOOK AT ME...

WHEN I WAS SEVEN, I USED TO DRESS UP IN SHEETS AND DREAM OF THE DAY I'D MARCH DOWN THE AISLE AND EVERYONE WOULD LOOK AT ME...

MY ENTIRE LIFE HAS BEEN SPENT PREPARING FOR THE DAY I'D MARCH DOWN THE AISLE AND EVERYONE WOULD LOOK AT ME.

WHAT'S WRONG?

I HAVE TO MARCH DOWN THE AISLE AND EVERYONE'S GOING TO LOOK AT ME!

ANOTHER FINELY HONED FEMALE SKILL TURNS ON US AT THE LAST MINUTE.

SIMON WILL NOW SAY A FEW SPECIAL WORDS...

I LOVE YOU, CHARLENE. IN A WORLD OF PLOTTING, MANIPULATIVE WOMEN, YOU'RE SO FREE OF ULTERIOR MOTIVES. I LOVE YOUR INNOCENCE...YOUR HONESTY...AND THE SWEET, NAIVE WAY YOU LET OUR RELATIONSHIP BECOME WHAT IT IS.

...AND NOW CHARLENE WILL SAY A FEW WORDS...

ANY GIRLFRIEND WHO OPENS HER MOUTH IS A DEAD WOMAN!!

AACK! THE LINE! I'M AT THE LINE! I CAN SEE THE ACTUAL LINE!!

WHAT LINE, CATHY?

HALF THE RELATIVES AT YOUR WEDDING ARE TRYING TO FIX ME UP, AND HALF AREN'T BECAUSE I LOOK TOO OLD. I'M AT THE EXACT BORDERLINE! THE LINE ON THE MAP!

ONE FOOT IS IN THE STATE OF DESIRABILITY AND ONE FOOT IS IN THE STATE OF DECAY!

FIND THE PHOTO-GRAPHER! I'M AN HISTORIC LANDMARK!

"MAID OF HONOR" MAY HAVE BEEN AN OVER-STATEMENT.

WASN'T THAT A BEAUTIFUL WEDDING, IRVING ??

OH, NO. HERE COMES THE PRESSURE.

THEY LOOKED SO HAPPY !

HERE COMES THE GUILT...

IT WAS SO INSPIRING !

HERE COME THE DEMANDS...

AAACK!

WASN'T THAT A BEAUTIFUL WEDDING, SWEETIE ??

OH, NO. HERE COMES THE PRESSURE.

LOOK AT ALL THE DECORATIONS, CHARLENE !

57 SEPARATE TRIPS TO THE WEDDING PLANNER'S...

WHERE DID ALL THIS FOOD COME FROM ??

450 CALLS TO THE CATERER...

LOOK ! THERE'S A CAKE, A BAND, FLOWERS !!

TWO NERVOUS BREAKDOWNS AND NINE PULVERIZED VACATION DAYS...

ISN'T IT GREAT HOW IT ALL JUST KIND OF CAME TOGETHER ?? WE'LL HAVE TO HAVE A LOT OF PARTIES !

WHY BRIDES CONTINUE TO WEEP AFTER THE WEDDING.

...BUT I LIKE BEING SINGLE... I LOVE LIVING ALONE...I'M....

Charlene and Simon

YOU DON'T HAVE TO DEFEND YOURSELF TO THIS BUSYBODY, CATHY.

Charlene and Simon

EVERYONE GETS SO MARRIAGE-CRAZY AT A WEDDING ! WHY SHOULD YOU HAVE TO EXPLAIN YOUR CHOICE TO LIVE A PERFECTLY HAPPY, FULFILLING SINGLE LIFE TO ANYONE ??!

...AND YOU MUST BE HER MOTHER ??

IT HAD NOTHING TO DO WITH HER UPBRINGING !!

Charlene and Simon

47

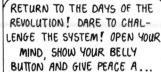

48

SLOUCHY SHOULDERS...
RUMPLED SKIRTS...
SHRUNKEN SWEATERS...
BAGGY WAISTS...
ANCIENT FLORALS...
COBWEB LACE...

PUT IT ALL TOGETHER WITH A KLUNKY SHOE AND CROCHETED BEANIE, AND WE REDEFINE FEMININITY FOR THE '90s!

THE POWER WAIF.

HERE. YOU'LL WANT THE MATCHING MACRAMÉ TOTE SO YOU CAN CARRY A CHANGE OF CLOTHES.

SUPPORT OF THE DIET SODA INDUSTRY, PROVIDING MILLIONS OF NEEDED JOBS!

NOT DEDUCTIBLE.

PERSONAL FUNDING OF THE GREETING CARD, BEAUTY SUPPLY AND MICROWAVE POPCORN BUSINESSES!

NOT DEDUCTIBLE.

EXPENSES INCURRED TRYING TO SEDUCE A HUSBAND, WHICH COULD LEAD TO CHILDREN AND A NEW GENERATION OF TAXPAYERS!

NOT DEDUCTIBLE.

ONCE AGAIN, THE GOVERNMENT FAILS TO SUPPORT THE CREATIVE ARTS.

I TRIED TO LOWER YOUR TAXES, CATHY, BUT THERE'S NOTHING I CAN DO.

ACCOUNTANT

THERE ARE NO LOOPHOLES ANYMORE. THERE ARE NO BREAKS. MY HANDS ARE TIED.

THERE'S NOTHING ANYONE CAN DO! WE'RE ALL IN THE SAME BOAT! YOU AND I ARE IN THE EXACT SAME BOAT!

...EXCEPT NOW YOU OWE ME $350.

ANOTHER NAUSEATING SPRING CRUISE ON THE GOOD SHIP C.P.A.

ACCOUNTANT

THIS YEAR YOUR TAX DOLLARS WILL BE USED TO FUND THE I.R.S. OFFICE THAT GIVES FREE TAX-RETURN ADVICE TO THE MEMBERS OF CONGRESS WHO WROTE THE TAX LAWS.

I BEG YOUR PARDON?

THE PEOPLE WHO WROTE THE TAX LAWS ARE TOO CONFUSED TO DO THEIR OWN TAXES... BUT THE ONES WHO TRY GET SPECIAL HELP, THANKS TO YOU.

ACCOUNTANT

I WORKED ALL YEAR SO THE AUTHORS OF THE TAX LAWS CAN GET FREE HELP UNDERSTANDING THEIR OWN IDIOTIC FORMS?? IS THERE NO COMPASSION FOR THE INDIVIDUAL??!

NONSENSE. THEY WERE JUST SICK ABOUT YOUR PUNY RAISE. THEY WERE COUNTING ON EXTRA TAXES FROM YOU TO REDECORATE THE LOBBY.

ACCOUNTANT

ATTENTION ALL EMPLOYEES: FRANK, WHO NEEDS TWENTY PAGES TYPED, HAS JUST GIVEN ME A PLASTIC DESK PLAQUE FOR SECRETARIES' WEEK!

...TOM HAS JUST ONE-UPPED THE PLAQUE WITH A BOUQUET OF ROSES... PHIL HAS JUST TOPPED THE ROSES WITH A SILVER BROOCH... BRIAN HAS JUST OUSTED THE BROOCH WITH A SOLID GOLD BRACELET!

THE BRACELET IS THE ONE TO BEAT! ANYONE WHO WANTS ANY WORK DONE WILL HAVE TO BEAT A SOLID GOLD BRACELET!

UNDERPAY ME IF YOU MUST. UNDERESTIMATE ME IF YOU DARE.

I HOPE YOU'LL JOIN US FOR SECRETARIES' WEEK LUNCH, ANDREA.

I'M NOT A SECRETARY, AND EVEN IF I WERE, I'D HAVE NO PART IN AN EVENT THAT MAKES AMENDS FOR A PUNY SALARY WITH A FREE LUNCH.

EVERY WOMAN WHO REFUSES TO BE BOUGHT OFF WITH A FANCY MEAL SENDS A MESSAGE TO THE COMPANY ABOUT HER REAL VALUE!

I'M UP ANOTHER $5.50!

I DIDN'T HAVE TIME TO GET YOU A SECRETARIES' WEEK GIFT, CHARLENE.

OH, MR. PINKLEY, I KNOW HOW BUSY YOU ARE!

AFTER ALL, IT IS I WHO DEALS WITH YOUR PHONE CALLS... YOUR PAPERS... YOUR CLIENTS... IT IS I WHO TRIES TO BUFFER YOU FROM THE CHAOS, EVEN AS I WORK INTO THE WEE HOURS, PRAYING THAT I CAN LESSEN THE STRAIN OF YOUR BUSY, IMPORTANT LIFE!

OH, FOR CRYING OUT LOUD! CHARGE YOURSELF SOMETHING FROM A GIFT CATALOG!

FROM A BUSINESS SCHOOL DIPLOMA, A DOCTORATE IN GUILT.

ANDREA IS COMPLETELY OFFENDED BY SECRETARIES' WEEK... CHARLENE CONSIDERS IT A RELIGIOUS HOLIDAY...

ANDREA SAYS ANY MENTION OF IT IS DEMEANING... CHARLENE WANTS A PARADE THROWN IN HER HONOR...

WHO DO I BELIEVE? WHAT AM I SUPPOSED TO DO?? HELP ME, CATHY!!

I'LL GO TELL ALL THE WOMEN IN THE WORLD TO START AGREEING WITH EACH OTHER IF YOU'LL GO TELL ALL THE MEN THAT NO ONE REALLY HAS THIGHS LIKE CINDY CRAWFORD.

WHO WAS THAT WHO ANSWERED YOUR PHONE, CHARLENE?

THAT WAS SIMON, MY HUSBAND!

IS HE STILL THERE?

OH, YES. HE'S STANDING RIGHT HERE!

WHEN'S HE GOING TO LEAVE SO WE CAN TALK?

HE ISN'T GOING TO LEAVE, SILLY! HE'S MY HUSBAND!

CHARLENE... I NEED TO TALK TO YOU ABOUT IRVING!

GREAT. MAYBE MY HUSBAND CAN OFFER SOME INSIGHT FROM THE MALE POINT OF VIEW.

LEAVE IT TO A MARRIAGE TO RUIN A RELATIONSHIP.

I HAVE TO FIND OUT WHAT'S GOING ON IN RUSSIA...

I HAVE TO KNOW WHAT'S GOING ON IN BOSNIA... I HAVE TO READ EVERY DETAIL OF WHAT'S GOING ON IN THE MIDDLE EAST!

WHAT'S GOING ON WITH US, HONEY?

HUH?

AS USUAL, THE ONLY REAL FOREIGN TURF IS SITTING RIGHT HERE NEXT TO HIM ON THE COUCH.

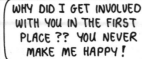

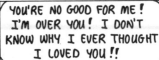

WHEN I WAS YOUNG AND SINGLE, THE WORST MEN SEEMED PERFECT TO ME.

CLEAN POLICY

NOW I'M OLD AND SINGLE AND EVEN THE GOOD ONES LOOK SO STRANGE.

THAT'S BECAUSE THERE'S A STIGMA ATTACHED TO WOMEN WHO REACH OUR AGE AND HAVE NEVER MARRIED. THE STIGMA AFFECTS WHAT YOU PROJECT... THE STIGMA AFFECTS HOW MEN RESPOND... AND THE STIGMA AFFECTS HOW YOU RESPOND TO HOW THEY RESPOND.

NOW THAT I'M NOT LOOKING FOR LOVE IN ALL THE WRONG PLACES, I'M TRYING TO SEE IT WITH AN ASTIGMATISM.

CLEANUP POLICY

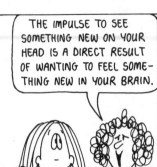

THE PROBLEM WITH YOUNG PEOPLE IS THAT YOU SUBSTITUTE TV FOR REAL RELATIONSHIPS.

YOU SIT LIKE BLOBS, FEELING CLOSER TO TV CHARACTERS THAN TO PEOPLE IN YOUR OWN LIVES, AND WHEN THE SHOW IS CANCELED, YOU FEEL DESERTED.

IT'S TIME TO TURN OFF THE TV AND BECOME A FULL, ACTIVE, INVOLVED PARTICIPANT IN A RELATIONSHIP YOU KNOW WILL ALWAYS BE THERE FOR YOU!

THE TRASHY ROMANCE NOVEL!!

AT LEAST THERE WILL BE SOME EYE MOVEMENT.

THAT'S WHO YOU WANTED ME TO MEET?? ARE YOU OUT OF YOUR MIND??

DO YOU KNOW **NOTHING** ABOUT ME?? ARE YOU COMPLETELY OBLIVIOUS TO MY SUPERIOR STANDARDS??

HOW DESPERATE DO YOU THINK I AM, ANYWAY??

WHY THEY CALL IT MARRIED "LIFE," BUT CALL IT THE DATING "SCENE."

I HEAR YOU MET SOMEONE NEW, SWEETIE.

WHAT ARE YOU TALKING ABOUT, MOM??

CHARLENE'S MOTHER-IN-LAW MENTIONED IT TO HER NEIGHBOR RUTH, WHO TOLD JOYCE, WHO TOLD GLADYS, WHO TOLD MARTHA...

MARTHA RELAYED IT TO DOROTHY WHO CALLED JUNE WHO CALLED ESTHER WHO CALLED DORIS WHO TOLD FRAN WHO BLABBED IT TO FLO, WHO CAME RUNNING TO ME.

MY MOTHER. LIFETIME MEMBER OF THE OLD GIRL'S NETWORK.

SOMETHING I CAN HELP YOU FIND?

ME?? OH, NO! NO THANKS!

SOME **SPECIAL NEW STYLE**??

NO! NOTHING SPECIAL!

SOME **UNIQUE FEATURE**??

NO! GO AWAY! I DON'T NEED HELP! I KNOW WHAT I'M LOOKING FOR!

THE SUITS THAT INFLATE TO GIVE THE ILLUSION OF A BUST ARE OVER THERE!!

LEAVE IT TO THE SWIMWEAR INDUSTRY TO FIND A WAY TO HUMILIATE ME BEFORE I EVEN GET TO THE DRESSING ROOM.

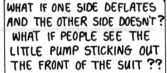

66

OH, MISS? THE SIZE 5 SWIMSUIT IS BAGGY IN THE REAR AND THE TOP IS TOO SMALL FOR MY WELL-PROPORTIONED CHEST!

DON'T YOU HAVE ANYTHING THAT SHOWS OFF MY CLEAVAGE WITHOUT ALL THIS CUMBERSOME PADDING??

BRING IN SOME SEXIER BIKINIS... MAYBE SOMETHING IN A TEENSY WHITE MACRAMÉ THONG?!

VERY HUMOROUS.

I'VE GIVEN UP ON MY OWN DAY AND AM DOING WHAT I CAN TO RUIN EVERYONE ELSE'S.

67

COME ONE! COME ALL! COME TO ME, DEMORALIZED BATHING SUIT SHOPPERS!

SHOES

LOOK AT YOUR PERFECT LITTLE FEET! LOOK AT YOUR SLENDER, LEAN, MUSCLE-TONED FEET!

SHOES

FLAUNT THAT CURVY HEEL! SHOW OFF THAT FABULOUS ARCH! WOW THEM WITH YOUR SASSY PEEKABOO TOES! EVERY SINGLE STYLE LOOKS INCREDIBLE ON THOSE SEXY, SLIM, TRIM, ONE HUNDRED PERCENT CELLULITE-FREE FEET!

IN WINTER, WE'RE A SHOE DEPARTMENT. IN SUMMER, WE'RE A SELF-RESPECT REDEMPTION CENTER.

SHOES

I GRABBED A BATHING SUIT OFF THE RACK.

I SEARCHED FOUR MALLS IN THREE COUNTIES FOR A BATHING SUIT.

I BOUGHT THE FIRST ONE I SAW IN MY SIZE.

I MODELED 100 SUITS IN EVERY MIRROR FROM EVERY ANGLE IN EVERY POSSIBLE LIGHTING SITUATION.

I THREW MINE IN A DRAWER WHEN I GOT HOME.

I BUILT A WHOLE NEW DIET AND WORKOUT PROGRAM AROUND MINE AND PLEDGED A LIFETIME OF COMMITMENT AND SACRIFICE.

MEN SHOW UP. WOMEN MAKE IT A RELATIONSHIP.

INNOCENCE

A SWIMSUIT ON THE BODY AND ICE CREAM IN EACH HAND.

WISDOM

A SWIMSUIT ON THE BODY AND ICE CREAM IN THE REFRIGERATOR.

MATURITY

ICE CREAM IN THE BODY AND A SWIMSUIT ON THE REFRIGERATOR.

WE DON'T KNOW WHEN IT START-ED, BUT IT WAS SMASHED INTO FOCUS BY THE BREAKUP OF CHARLES AND DI... SEALED BY THE DEMISE OF THE SEARS CATALOG... AND CEMENTED BY THE CANCELLATION OF "CHEERS."

SUDDENLY EVERYTHING FEELS SO TEMPORARY, SO TRANSIENT. WE LONG FOR SOMETHING REAL, SOMETHING SOLID... A SAFE BET, A SURE THING, A KNOWN ENTITY... SOMETHING THAT JUST WON'T GO AWAY.

...AND SO CONTINUES THE THIRD STRAIGHT WEEK OF COMMENTARY ON THE PRESI-DENT'S #200 HAIRCUT...

RIDICULING WORLD LEADERS: THE PASSION THAT NEVER DIES.

FOUR NEW SOCIALLY RELEVANT, FAMILY-ORIENTED SHOWS: BEGUN, TRIED AND CAN-CELLED... SEVEN NEW POLI-TICALLY CORRECT, ETHNICALLY DIVERSE SHOWS: BEGUN, TRIED AND CANCELED.

EIGHT NEW GLOBALLY CON-CERNED, VIEWER-FRIENDLY, SEXUALLY SAFE, ENLIGHTENED ROLE MODEL SHOWS: BEGUN, TRIED AND CANCELED.

TV FINALLY SUCCEEDS AT MIRRORING REAL LIFE.

IT'S HARD TO FIND A RELA-TIONSHIP THAT LASTS MORE THAN THIRTEEN EPISODES.

VINTAGE CLOTHING...
RETRO FURNITURE...
OLDIES STATIONS...
DINER FOOD...
CLASSIC TOYS...
REMADE MOVIES...
RESTAGED PLAYS...
REVIVAL MUSICALS...
REUNION TOURS...

FRIED BY THE PRESENT AND FREAKED OUT BY THE FUTURE, AMERICA HUNGERS FOR THE ONE THING WE KNOW WE CAN TRUST AND DEPEND ON...

#95 FOR A PAIR OF USED COWBOY BOOTS??!

...THE COMFORTING SHRIEK OF OUR MOTHER'S VOICE.

THE MORE BLEAK THE FUTURE SEEMS, THE MORE PEOPLE CLING TO THE PAST, MOM.

NONSENSE. NOSTALGIA IS JUST A FAD.

LOOK AROUND! PEOPLE ARE DRESSING LIKE THE '60s... WATCHING TV SHOWS FROM THE '50s... REMAKING MOVIES FROM THE '40s... EVERYONE'S TERRIFIED OF THE FUTURE.

WELL, THERE'S NOTHING TO WORRY ABOUT, CATHY. THE FUTURE IS IN THE HANDS OF THE CHILDREN.

THE CHILDREN ARE ALL CLUTCHING DINOSAURS!!

I PUT ON MY $85 PRE-SHREDDED JEANS AND MY $130 WEATHERED DENIM SHIRT...

...KICK MY $15 NATTY SLOUCHED SOCKS ON MY $400 DISTRESSED-OAK TABLE...LEAN BACK ON MY $150 FACTORY-FADED THROW PILLOW...

...CLICK ON MY $350 STEREOPHONIC COLOR TV TO WATCH MONO-SOUND, BLACK-AND-WHITE "I LOVE LUCY" RERUNS...AND DREAM OF A SIMPLER, HAPPIER TIME...

...WHEN I HAD SOME MONEY.

I KNOW YOU'RE SWAMPED TODAY, BUT I JUST THOUGHT I'D CALL AND SAY HI, SWEETIE.

HI, MOM. I'M SWAMPED.

OH, I KNOW YOU DON'T HAVE TIME TO CHAT. I JUST WANTED TO SEE HOW YOU'RE DOING.

I DON'T HAVE TIME TO CHAT, MOM.

OOPS. I KNEW I WAS CALLING AT THE WORST POSSIBLE MOMENT. I'LL LET YOU GET BACK TO YOUR BUSY, IMPORTANT LIFE.

MOTHER

FOR EVERY PERFECTLY TIMED ANNOYING INTERRUPTION, THERE'S A HALF-HOUR GUILT-FOLLOW-UP CALL TO COME.

IT WAS SEEMING PRETTY FUTILE, CATHY. I ADMIT IT. I THOUGHT IT WAS ALL OVER.

...BUT I FORCED MYSELF TO READ A BOOK... I WATCHED A VIDEO... I TRIED LISTENING INSTEAD OF KNOWING IT ALL...

I REINVESTED MY HEART IN IT, AND NOT ONLY REMEMBERED WHY I FELL IN LOVE IN THE FIRST PLACE, BUT DISCOVERED A WHOLE NEW DEPTH OF COMMITMENT I NEVER THOUGHT POSSIBLE!

THE GOOD NEWS IS HE'S LEARNING HOW TO MAKE A RELATIONSHIP LAST. THE BAD NEWS IS IT'S WITH HIS GOLF GAME.

46% OF A MAN'S BRAIN IS IN LOVE WITH BUSINESS. I ACCEPT AND RESPECT THAT.

COSMETICS

32% OF HIS BRAIN IS IN LOVE WITH SPORTS... 21% OF HIS BRAIN IS IN LOVE WITH NEWS AND POLITICS...

THAT ONLY LEAVES ONE BRAIN CELL, MOM! WOMEN TODAY ARE COMPETING FOR ONE MISERABLE BRAIN CELL!

AND IT'S THE ONE WAY IN THE BACK. YOU NEED A NICE BIG BOTTLE OF COLOGNE.

DO YOU HAVE ANY THAT SMELLS LIKE POT ROAST? THAT'S HOW I REELED HER FATHER IN.

IF THINGS AREN'T WORKING WITH IRVING, MRS. JOHNSTON'S NEPHEW MIGHT STILL BE AVAILABLE, CATHY.

FINE. FIX ME UP, MOM.

FIX YOU UP??

FIX ME UP. WHY NOT?

I'M OLD. I'M BITTER. I'M BEATEN. I'M DISGUSTED. I FLING MYSELF FROM ONE PATHETIC RUT TO ANOTHER. FIX ME UP, MOM! HOW MUCH WORSE COULD IT GET??

THEY ALWAYS TURN TO MOTHER FOR THE FINISHING TOUCHES.

74

YOUNG PEOPLE ARE TOO PICKY. I'M SURE MRS. JOHNSTON'S NEPHEW WILL BE A WONDERFUL MATCH FOR YOU, CATHY.

...BUT WAIT. MAYBE FLO'S COUSIN'S NEIGHBOR IS BETTER. ....WAIT. MARTHA'S ACCOUNTANT IS SUPPOSED TO BE CUTE...

...MAYBE THERE'S SOMEONE BETTER OUT THERE I HAVEN'T HEARD OF YET! **WAIT!** I HAVE TO GO MINGLE! I HAVE TO LOITER IN FRONT OF DOCTORS' BUILDINGS!! **MAYBE IT'S NOT TOO LATE FOR THE CROWN PRINCE NARUHITO!!**

FUNNY HOW MUCH BETTER WE UNDERSTAND THE JELLO WHEN WE'VE SEEN THE MOLD.

BE UP. BE OPEN. BE INTERESTED.

TRY. MAKE AN EFFORT. GIVE IT A CHANCE. SEE WHERE IT GOES. JUST TRY. SMILE AND TRY.

DING DONG

YAP YAP

UH, OH! N.G.! I'M A CAT PERSON!

NEXT.

HI! I'M BRADLEY! '90s MAN! PECS OF STEEL, HEART OF GOLD, PORCELAIN CAPS, AND PREVENTATIVE HAIR LOSS TREATMENT HAS ALREADY BEGUN!

DRUG-FREE, NICOTINE-FREE, CAFFEINE-FREE, ALCOHOL-FREE, DISEASE-FREE, DELUSION-FREE!

I LOVE ROOMY JEANS, CUSHY CARS, JUMBO SCREENS AND WOMEN WHO AREN'T AFRAID TO POP THE BIG QUESTION!

WILL YOU EXCUSE ME WHILE I GO THROW UP?

HA, HA! WHAT A KIDDER! YES, I **AM** WEARING CALVIN KLEIN UNDERWEAR!

77

WHAT? WHAT IS THIS? GET OFF MY WAIST, FROZEN YOGURT! IF I'D WANTED SOMETHING ON MY WAIST, I WOULD HAVE EATEN ICE CREAM!

AND YOU! GET AWAY FROM MY THIGHS, RICE CAKES! I CAN'T BELIEVE YOU HAD THE NERVE TO HANG AROUND!

I WANT ALL FAT-FREE GRANOLA CRUMBS, ALL LOW-FAT CHEESE PUFFS, AND EACH AND EVERY DISAPPOINTING LITTLE FRUIT JUICE BAR TO PACK YOUR THINGS AND MOVE OUT OF THE HIP AREA IMMEDIATELY!!!

WANT TO ORDER LUNCH, CATHY?

NO, THANKS. I'M STILL BUSY ORDERING MY SNACKS FROM LAST NIGHT.

HAVE YOU TALKED TO YOUR BLIND DATE SINCE LAST WEEK, CATHY?

NO! I HOPE I NEVER TALK TO HIM! I WOULD NEVER CALL HIM! HIM?? BLEAH! NO!!

...BUT WHAT IF HE THINKS HE'S NOT CALLING ME?? WHAT IF HE'S TAKING CREDIT FOR REJECTING ME WHEN, IN FACT, I'M REJECTING HIM??

I MUST CALL! I MUST CALL AND MAKE SURE HE KNOWS THAT UNDER NO CIRCUMSTANCES WOULD I EVER EVER EVER EVER EVEN THINK OF CALLING HIM!!

HELLO, BRADLEY?!

THE WOMEN ALWAYS CRACK FIRST.

I WAS ANNOYED THAT YOU MEDDLED IN MY LOVE LIFE, MOM... BUT ON THE OTHER HAND, IT GAVE ME PERSPECTIVE.

I WAS IRKED THAT YOU BUTTED IN... BUT ON THE OTHER HAND, IT FORCED ME TO TAKE CHARGE.

EVERY SINGLE TIME YOU DO SOMETHING AGGRAVATING, I GET INFUSED WITH A NEW DETERMINATION THAT HAS A POSITIVE RIPPLE EFFECT ON EVERY OTHER THING I DO!

MOM: THE BINDING ELEMENT IN THE MEATLOAF OF LIFE.

I WORK HARD, PLAY ROUGH, INVEST IN LONG-TERM GROWTH STOCKS AND PRE-RUMPLED KHAKI LEISURE WEAR.

I CAN QUOTE U2, SING SPRINGSTEEN, DO THE ACHY-BREAKY, RUN WINDOWS, LIFT MY WEIGHT, PROGRAM MY VCR, AND WEEP IN PUBLIC!

I'VE BEATEN A SOUFFLÉ IN THE KITCHEN, A DRUM IN THE WOODS, MY HEAD AGAINST THE WALL... ...AND NOW I'M READY TO SNUGGLE UP WITH A SPECIAL LADY AND START CREATING LITTLE TINY VERSIONS OF MYSELF!

WHILE THE CITY SLEEPS, ANOTHER SINGLE WOMAN GATHERS MATERIAL FOR HER NOVEL.

YOU'RE TAKING NOTES! INCREDIBLE! AM I ON TONIGHT, OR WHAT?!

IT'S A BEAUTIFUL SUMMER EVENING. I SHOULD GO FOR A LONG WALK.

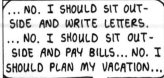

...NO. I SHOULD SIT OUTSIDE AND WRITE LETTERS. ...NO. I SHOULD SIT OUTSIDE AND PAY BILLS... NO. I SHOULD PLAN MY VACATION...

...NO. I SHOULD GO MEET SOMEONE AND THEN PLAN A VACATION... NO. I SHOULD REORGANIZE MY CLOSET SO I'LL BE READY FOR A VACATION... NO. I SHOULD RETHINK MY CAREER. I CAN'T AFFORD A VACATION... NO. I SHOULD READ A BOOK. JUST RELAX AND READ... NO. I SHOULD WORK OUT, THEN RELAX AND REA

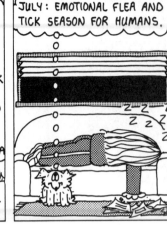

JULY: EMOTIONAL FLEA AND TICK SEASON FOR HUMANS.

UNBELIEVABLE. I'VE ALREADY SEEN THIS EPISODE.

THERE HAVE BEEN 200 EPISODES OF THIS SHOW... I'VE ONLY SEEN IT ONE OTHER TIME... AND YOU'RE RERUNNING THE EXACT SAME EPISODE I ALREADY SAW!!

HOW DID YOU KNOW?? WHY ARE YOU TORTURING ME?? WHERE ARE THE 199 OTHER EPISODES NOW THAT I'M READY AND WILLING TO HAVE MY SENSES DULLED BY YOUR STUPID PROGRAM?!!

IF IT ISN'T VIOLENCE ON TV, IT'S VIOLENCE AT TV.

I'M TURNING INTO MY MOTHER... SENSIBLE... PREDICTABLE... VALUE-CONSCIOUS ...OLD-FASHIONED... BORING...

snip!

I WANT TO BE EXOTIC! I CAN BE EXOTIC! I CAN PUSH THE BOUNDS! I CAN LIVE ON THE WILD SIDE! HA, HA! STAND BACK, WORLD!

ANOTHER SATURDAY NIGHT METAMORPHOSIS: FROM BETTY CROCKER TO LADY GODIVA.

GODIVA CHOCOLATE

HOW WAS YOUR WEEKEND, ANDREA?

WEEK-END??

WE HAD 12 POTTY TRAINING ACCIDENTS, TWO RUNS TO THE EMERGENCY ROOM, AND ONE PSYCHODRAMA AT TOYS 'R' US.

I DID NINE LOADS OF LAUNDRY, COOKED TEN MEALS, CHANGED 37 DIAPERS, MADE FOUR TRIPS TO THE GROCERY STORE, AND FRANTICALLY TRIED TO PICK UP THE DEBRIS WHILE LUKE TOOK THE KIDS ON DESPERATION CAR RIDES TRYING TO GET THEM TO GO TO SLEEP.

GEE... SORRY I DIDN'T CALL. I GOT SO BUSY.

DOING WHAT?!!

IT'S SO HARD TO GET OUT OF THE HOUSE IN THE MORNING, CATHY.

WHEW... I KNOW WHAT YOU MEAN, ANDREA.

I MEAN, I'M SURE MY CHILDREN WILL BE OK. THEY'LL BE FINE. MILLIONS OF MOTHERS WORK. IT'S GOOD FOR KIDS TO SEE THEIR MOTHERS WORK.

I'M A GOOD ROLE MODEL. MY TIME WITH THEM IS BETTER BECAUSE I'M NOT WITH THEM ALL THE TIME. WE NEED THE MONEY. I HAVE NO CHOICE. THEY KNOW I LOVE THEM. THEY'LL BE OK. I HOPE THEY'LL BE OK. I HOPE I'M DOING THE RIGHT THING.... AM I DOING THE RIGHT THING??

NOTHING LIKE A WORKING MOM TO SNAP THE OLD, "DID I WEAR THE RIGHT LIP GLOSS" DEBATE INTO PERSPECTIVE.

DO I HEAR TV IN THE BACKGROUND, HONEY?? WE SAID NO TV FOR THE KIDS.

NO TV UNLESS THEY SCREAM, AND THEN A LITTLE TV.

A LITTLE TV BUT NO CARTOONS. JUST EDUCATIONAL.

JUST EDUCATIONAL UNLESS THEY'RE REALLY WILD, AND THEN ONE VIDEO.

ONE VIDEO UNLESS THEY'RE COMPLETELY BERSERK, AND THEN TWO VIDEOS.

TWO VIDEOS UNLESS WE JUST CAN'T TAKE IT, AND THEN THEY GET ANYTHING THEY WANT AND WE PLEDGE TO DO BETTER TOMORROW!

WE'VE MOVED BEYOND CO-PARENTING AND ARE INTO CO-DETERIORATING.

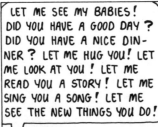

FOR ZENITH, WE PLAYED STRAVINSKI IN UTERO... FOR GUS, WE TRY TO KEEP THE VOLUME DOWN ON "HARD COPY".

FOR ZENITH, WE ENCOURAGED OPTIC-NERVE DEVELOPMENT WITH 17TH-CENTURY MASTER-PIECE FLASHCARDS...FOR GUS, WE TOSS A "MUTANT NINJA TURTLE" BOOK IN THE CRIB AND HOPE HE DOESN'T EAT IT.

FOR ZENITH, WE STIMULATED MOTOR SKILLS WITH STERILIZED GREEK ALPHABET FORMS...FOR GUS WE SCRAPE THE BANANA OFF THE REMOTE CONTROL.

OUR SON IS A PORTRAIT OF THE SECOND-CHILD SYNDROME!

HE WOULD BE, BUT NO ONE'S TAKEN HIS PICTURE IN FOUR MONTHS.

"MOTHERING YOUR KIDS"...
"THE EVOLVING MOTHER"...
"THE MOTHER BOND"...
"THE WORKING MOTHER"...
"MOTHERING RIGHT"...

"HOW TO FATHER"...
"THE BIRTH OF A FATHER"...
"FATHER POWER"...
"FATHERING IN THE '90s"...
"FATHERHOOD IN AMERICA"...

"THE JOY OF PARENTHOOD"...
"EVERYDAY PARENTING"...
"THE PARENT'S HANDBOOK"...
"HEALTHY PARENTING"...
"THE PARENT PARTNERSHIP"...

WHEW! THAT SHOULD SLOW THEM DOWN FOR A FEW MINUTES!

REMEMBER WHEN WE HAD THE ENERGY TO ACTUALLY READ??

BITING YOUR BABY BROTHER IS NOT ACCEPTABLE, ZENITH! YOU'RE HAVING A TIME OUT!

WAAH!

WAAH!

...BUT WHAT IF SHE BIT HIM TO EXPRESS HER ANGER AND HURT THAT I'M GONE AT WORK ALL DAY?

WHAT IF SHE SENSES MY SPECIAL FATHER-SON BOND, AND IS PLEADING FOR EQUAL ATTENTION?

I FEEL WE'RE REALLY COMING TOGETHER AS A FAMILY, HONEY.

ALL WE NEED IS FOR SOMEONE BESIDES US TO BE IN CHARGE.

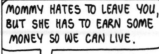

MOMMY'S GOING TO WORK NOW AND DADDY WILL TAKE CARE OF YOU.

OK. BYE.

MOMMY HATES TO LEAVE YOU, BUT SHE HAS TO EARN SOME MONEY SO WE CAN LIVE.

OK. BYE.

IT BREAKS MOMMY'S HEART TO GO! I'LL THINK ABOUT YOU EVERY MINUTE! I'LL MISS YOU EVERY SECOND! GOODBYE, MY SWEET BABIES, GOODBYE!!

NICE WORK, ANDREA.

CAN I HELP IT IF THEY GET EMOTIONAL ABOUT THEIR MOTHER?

...HUH?? I'M SORRY, MR. PINKLEY. I WAS THINKING ABOUT MY CHILDREN.

SEE, ANDREA? THIS IS WHY MOTHERS WILL NEVER MAKE IT IN BUSINESS.

PERHAPS SOMEONE WHO'S A LITTLE MORE FOCUSED ON THE CORPORATE AGENDA CAN CLARIFY THE POINT FOR US... ....ANYONE??

CALL IRVING OR DON'T CALL IRVING?

QUIT JOB OR DON'T QUIT JOB?

EAT DONUT OR DON'T EAT DONUT?

KEEP SHOES OR RETURN SHOES?

MARRY SUE OR DUMP SUE?

GROW MOUSTACHE OR DON'T GROW MOUSTACHE?

THAI FOR LUNCH OR PIZZA FOR LUNCH?

I CAN'T WAIT TO SEE YOU, IRVING... I WANT TO FORGET ANDREA AND HER KIDS... FORGET CHARLENE AND HER MARRIAGE... JUST BE WITH YOU... JUST YOU AND ME...

...BUT WHY AREN'T YOU INVOLVED WITH MY FRIENDS... WHY AREN'T YOU WORRYING ABOUT MARRIAGE AND CHILDREN... WHAT HAVE YOU BEEN DOING, ANYWAY???

WHY AM I ALWAYS COMING TO SEE YOU?? YOU SHOULD BE BEGGING TO COME SEE ME! YOU SHOULD WORSHIP ME! WHAT'S WRONG WITH YOU?? WHY DO I EVEN LIKE YOU??!!

MORE PROOF THAT PEOPLE MOVE IN TOGETHER BECAUSE THE RELATIONSHIP CAN NO LONGER SURVIVE THE DRIVE OVER.

IRVING?? OPEN UP!!

BAM BAM

BY OPENING UP MY GENTLE, NURTURING SIDE, A FRIEND HELPED ME SEE HOW MUCH I MISSED YOU, CATHY.

WHAT DID SHE DO TO YOU, IRVING?

SHE DOESN'T MATTER. I'VE COME BACK TO YOU!

I NEED TO KNOW WHAT SHE DID. WHAT DID SHE SAY? WHAT DID SHE WEAR? HOW DID SHE ACT??

FORGET HER, HONEY. I'M HERE! I WANT TO TALK ABOUT US!

WHAT WORKED ON YOU?? I HAVE TO KNOW WHAT WORKED ON YOU!!

MONTHS OF WAITING FOR MY SWEETHEART TO COME BACK, AND ALL I REALLY WANT FROM HIM IS THE OTHER WOMAN'S PHONE NUMBER.

MY HAIR WILL WORK TODAY... SOMETHING IN MY CLOSET WILL LOOK GREAT...MY MAKEUP WILL COME OUT EXACTLY THE WAY IT DID THE ONE TIME IT LOOKED PERFECT...

MY THIGHS WILL HAVE SHRUNK IN THE NIGHT... I WON'T HAVE TO ROOT THROUGH THE DISH-WASHER FOR A SEMI-CLEAN COFFEE MUG, OR THE LAUNDRY BASKET FOR UNDERWEAR... ...I WILL BE ABLE TO GET READY IN 20 MINUTES INSTEAD OF THE FULL HOUR AND A HALF IT ALWAYS TAKES...

GETTING OUT OF BED: THE ULTIMATE LEAP OF FAITH.

THAT WILL BE $4.05.

LONG-DISTANCE CALLING CARD... INSTRUCTION CARD FOR LONG-DISTANCE CALLING CARD... ROAD SERVICE CARD... DISCOUNT WAREHOUSE CARD... VIDEO MEMBERSHIP CARD... CHECK CASHING CARD... ANSWERING MACHINE REMOTE PLAYBACK INSTRUCTION CARD...

HEALTH INSURANCE CARD... PRESCRIPTION CARD... BUSINESS CARD... ATM CARD... SOCIAL SECURITY CARD... HEALTH CLUB ID CARD... SECRET P.I.N. NUMBER CARD... CAR WASH GAME CARD... CAR INSURANCE CLAIMS PROCEDURE CARD...

EVERY YEAR IT TAKES A BIGGER WALLET TO HOLD LESS MONEY.

AUGUST 2:

FIVE PEOPLE ARE ON VACA-TION! IT'S IMPOSSIBLE!! IT'S A NIGHTMARE! CRISIS ALERT!! WE'RE RUINED!!

AUGUST 3:

FIVE PEOPLE ARE ON VACATION! WE'LL MAKE IT SOMEHOW! WE'LL ALL PULL TOGETHER!! WE'LL WORK THROUGH THE NIGHT!!

AUGUST 4:

FIVE PEOPLE ARE ON VACATION.. ...SO WHAT? HO, HUM. WHAT'S THE DIFFERENCE? LET IT SLIDE. IS ANYONE ORDERING LUNCH?

IT ALWAYS TAKES HIM THE FIRST FEW DAYS TO UNWIND.

JOHN, MARTHA AND TONY ARE ON VACATION AND, THEREFORE, USELESS.

JOAN, HELEN AND MIKE HAVE JUST RETURNED FROM VACATION AND ARE, THEREFORE, USELESS...ROBERT, BRIAN AND LISA ARE ABOUT TO GO ON VACATION AND ARE USELESS.

I ALONE AM FUNCTIONING BECAUSE I HAVEN'T EVEN THOUGHT ABOUT WHERE I'M GOING OR WHO I'M GOING WITH EVEN THOUGH MY VACATION STARTS IN A WEEK!

GOD BLESS THE SINGLE PEOPLE.

HAVE TO HAVE IT... HAVE TO HAVE IT... HAVE TO HAVE IT...

SALES

HAVE TO GET RID OF IT... HAVE TO GET RID OF IT... HAVE TO GET RID OF IT...

RETURNS

HAVE TO HAVE IT... HAVE TO HAVE IT... HAVE TO HAVE IT...

SALES

HAVE TO GET RID OF IT...HAVE TO GET RID OF IT...HAVE TO GET RID OF IT...

RETURNS

HAVE TO HAVE IT... HAVE TO HAVE IT... HAVE TO HAVE IT...

SALES

THE BINGE AND PURGE APPROACH TO FASHION.

THE HAT AT THE STORE:

FABULOUS! SEXY! SOPHISTICATED!

THE HAT AT HOME:

INCREDIBLE! EXOTIC! ENTICING!

THE HAT IN THE CAR:

HOT! HOT! HOT!

THE HAT IN PUBLIC:

RELAX! TAKE OFF YOUR HAT! ENJOY YOURSELF!

COLORADO RIVER RAFTING! THIS LOOKS FUN!

I JUST SPENT THE MORNING RESEARCHING QUAINT INNS IN MAINE FOR YOU.

TRAVEL

SANTA FE! HOW MUCH IS IT TO GO TO SANTA FE?

I SPENT YESTERDAY TRYING TO FIND YOU A CHEAP FARE TO HAWAII!

WAIT!... I ALWAYS WANTED TO SEE MEXICO!

I HAVE A RENTAL CAR ON HOLD FOR YOU IN ROME!

...I'M SORRY. LET'S JUST STOP, TAKE A DEEP BREATH AND FOCUS ON THE MAIN QUESTION.

THANK YOU.

VEL

DO I HAVE ENOUGH BONUS MILES FOR AUSTRALIA?

WHO REFERRED YOU TO MY OFFICE?!!

TRAVEL

MANY SINGLE TRAVELERS FIND THAT TOUR GROUPS ARE A GREAT PLACE TO MEET SOMEONE.

WHO ELSE WILL BE THERE?

TRAVEL

I BEG YOUR PARDON?

I NEED A COMPLETE RUNDOWN ON EVERYONE ON THE TOUR SO I CAN TELL IF THERE'S ANYONE I WANT TO MEET OR IF THE VACATION WOULD BE A COMPLETE WASTE.

YOU WANT TO PRE-REJECT YOUR CO-TRAVELERS?

BETTER TO DO IT NOW THAN TO PAY A FORTUNE AND REJECT THEM ALL IN THE BOARDING AREA!

PERHAPS YOU'RE NOT THE TOUR GROUP TYPE. HOW ABOUT A NICE SOLO FLIGHT TO EUROPE?

WHO ELSE WILL BE THERE?

TRAVEL

HOW MUCH WOULD IT HAVE BEEN IF I'D BOUGHT THE TICKETS THREE MONTHS AGO?

YOU DON'T WANT TO KNOW.

TRAVEL

YES I DO. I WANT TO KNOW HOW MUCH CHEAPER IT COULD HAVE BEEN.

YOU REALLY DON'T WANT TO KNOW.

YES I DO! I WANT TO KNOW HOW MUCH I'M SUFFERING!! I MUST KNOW TO THE PENNY HOW BADLY I BLEW IT THIS TIME!!

AACK!!

CURIOSITY: THE FOUNDATION OF ALL TRAVEL THRILLS.

TRAVEL

TRAVEL AGENT COUPS

I SENT A 150-PERSON CLUB ON A NINE-CITY TOUR OF FRANCE.

I SENT A FAMILY OF EIGHT ON A MONTH-LONG TRIP TO ITALY.

I SENT TWELVE COUPLES ON A FIRST-CLASS TRIP TO THE ORIENT.

I SENT HER TO A DIFFERENT TRAVEL AGENT!!

HAH! I'LL JUST TAKE MY 47 POTENTIAL ITINERARIES ELSEWHERE!

MY VACATION STARTS IN A WEEK AND I HAVE NO ONE TO GO WITH.

CHARLENE HAS HER HUSBAND... ANDREA HAS HER FAMILY... SUE HAS HER BOYFRIEND... IRVING HAS GOLF...AND MY DOG ISN'T WELCOME IN HOTELS...

I HAVE NO ONE... I HAVE NOTHING... I'M ALL ALONE... COMPLETELY, HOPELESSLY ALONE....

ANOTHER WOMAN PLUNGES TO THE DEPTHS AND FINDS HER MOTHER THERE HOLDING SNORKEL EQUIPMENT.

WHO'S UP FOR A CRUISE?!

A CRUISE?? GO ON A CRUISE WITH YOU, MOM?

OH, CATHY, IT WILL BE SO WONDERFUL!

WE'LL SIT FOR HOURS UNDER THE MOONLIGHT... WE'LL REDISCOVER EACH OTHER... WE'LL MAKE MEMORIES FOR THE REST OF OUR LIVES...

WE'LL TALK...WE'LL CRY... WE'LL SHARE OUR DEEPEST SECRETS...WE'LL LAUGH AT THINGS ONLY THE TWO OF US CAN UNDERSTAND....

1,500 DATES LATER, AND IT TURNS OUT THE ONLY PERSON WITH A REAL FLAIR FOR ROMANCE IS MY MOTHER.

PACKING FOR VACATION: THE 7:00 PM PHASE

SHORTS
TOPS
JEANS

PACKING FOR VACATION: THE 11:00 PM PHASE

COCKTAIL DRESS
SILK PANTS
SWIRLY SKIRT
MACRAMÉ TOP

PACKING FOR VACATION: THE 2:00 AM PHASE

BALL GOWN
SPANDEX MINI DRESS
RHINESTONED CAPE
FAUX EMERALDS
SEQUINED STOCKINGS
SATIN LOUNGEWEAR
LEOPARD-PRINT
THONG WORKOUT WEAR

IN THE WEE HOURS OF THE MORNING, ANOTHER WOMAN LOOKS DELUSION IN THE EYE AND STUFFS IT IN A SUITCASE.

DOESN'T CATHY EVER BRUSH YOU, ELECTRA? I'LL BRUSH YOU EVERY DAY WHILE SHE'S GONE!

SEE, CATHY? YOUR FATHER DOLES OUT GUILT JUST LIKE I DO!

WE'LL ORDER PIZZAS EVERY NIGHT AND RENT LASSIE VIDEOS! YES!!

SEE?! YOUR FATHER IS JUST AS OBSESSIVE AS I AM!!

LOOK AT HIM! YOUR FATHER IS JUST AS BERSERK AS I AM! YOU DIDN'T GET IT ALL FROM ME!! IT WASN'T ALL FROM ME!!!

HE MUST HAVE LEARNED IT FROM YOU, TOO.

A MOTHER CAN TAKE OFF HER CROWN, BUT SHE'LL NEVER BE RELIEVED OF HER THRONE.

WHERE'S YOUR LUGGAGE, MOM?

THIS IS IT.

THAT'S IT?? FOR A WEEK-LONG CRUISE??

THIS IS IT.

I STUFFED EVERYTHING ELSE I'LL NEED INTO BOXES, SNEAKED THEM TO THE POST OFFICE AND EXPRESS-MAILED THEM TO THE SHIP SO YOUR FATHER WOULDN'T CROAK WHEN HE SAW HOW MUCH I WAS TAKING.

YOU COULD LEARN A FEW THINGS ABOUT PACKING FROM YOUR MOTHER.

SHE NEVER CEASES TO INSPIRE ME, DAD.

DID CATHY PUT ON ENOUGH SUNSCREEN? IS SHE DRINKING ENOUGH FLUIDS? IS SHE BURNING HER EYEBALLS BY READING IN THE SUN?

DID SHE REMEMBER TO TURN OFF HER COFFEEPOT? DID SHE SHUT ALL HER WINDOWS? IS SHE FALLING BEHIND AT WORK BY TAKING THIS TRIP?

DOES SHE TAKE HER VITAMINS? DOES SHE FLOSS HER TEETH? IS SHE HAPPY? IS SHE HEALTHY? DID SHE LEAVE HER PURSE LYING OUT IN THE ROOM?

ARE YOU ASLEEP, MOM?

MOTHERS NEVER SLEEP. WE JUST WORRY LYING DOWN WITH OUR EYES SHUT.

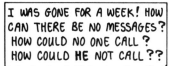

I WORKED LATE EVERY NIGHT THIS WEEK TO GET CAUGHT UP FROM MY ONE-WEEK VACATION.

I'LL WORK THE NEXT SIX WEEKENDS TO CATCH UP ON WHAT I'M LETTING SLIDE WHILE I'M TRYING TO GET CAUGHT UP... I'LL SPEND THE NEXT MONTH TRYING TO GET CAUGHT UP ON WHAT SLID WHILE I WAS CATCHING UP ON WHAT SLID.

ONE MEASLY FIVE-DAY FLING HAS SOMEHOW COMPOUNDED INTO AN ENDLESS SEA OF OBLIGATION!

FOR SOME, LIFE IMITATES ART. FOR ME, LIFE IMITATES CREDIT CARD DEBT.

OH, HORRORS! I HAVE THREE CHINS IN THIS PICTURE!

I HAVE A SHINY RED FACE AND MY HAIR IS STICKING STRAIGHT OUT!

WHAT'S THAT HANGING OUT OF MY DRESS??

MY THIGHS LOOK LIKE RAFTS!

AACK! THAT'S MY ARM!

LOOK AT THE GEEKY EXPRESSION ON MY FACE!

WE DO **NOT** LOOK THIS BAD!

WE DON'T LOOK LIKE THIS AT ALL!

WE HAVE NEVER LOOKED ANYTHING LIKE THIS!

SEVEN ROLLS OF FILM... 36 EXPOSURES PER ROLL... 252 PRINTS... AND NOT ONE RESEMBLES EITHER OF THE SUBJECTS.

YOU'RE FAT, ELECTRA, BUT IT'S JUST VACATION FAT. IT'S NEW FAT. END-OF-SUMMER FAT!

IT ISN'T **FAT** FAT YET! IT HASN'T SETTLED IN AND WELDED TO YOUR PERSONALITY! YOU STILL HAVE A CHANCE! THERE'S STILL TIME FOR YOU!

GET RID OF THE FAT **NOW**! GET RID OF THE FAT BEFORE IT UNPACKS ITS BAGS, HANGS ITS THINGS IN YOUR CLOSET AND **STARTS INVITING ALL ITS LITTLE FRIENDS OVER**!

EXPERIENCE COUNTS FOR NOTHING IN THE WORLD OF DIETING.

BEFORE YOU START A DIET YOU HAVE TO FACE REALITY, ELECTRA.

YOU HAVE TO GET ON THE SCALE AND TAKE A HARD, HONEST, PAINFUL LOOK AT THE TRUTH.

I WILL WEIGH US TOGETHER AND DIVIDE BY TWO!

NOTHING LIKE A MOTHER WHO'S WILLING TO SHARE THE LOAD...

"FEEDING A DOG FROM THE TABLE NOT ONLY PROMOTES OBESITY, BUT CAN ACTUALLY CONFUSE THE DOG'S STATUS..."

DOG CARE

"SINCE DOGS ARE PACK ANIMALS, THEY INSTINCTIVELY VIEW YOU AS THE PACK LEADER, AND WILL NOT QUESTION YOUR RIGHT TO EAT FIRST AND TO EAT BETTER FOOD..."

DOG

"A DOG SITTING UNDER THE TABLE BEGGING FOR SCRAPS IS AN INEXCUSABLE SIGN THAT YOU HAVE ALLOWED THE PACK STRUCTURE TO WEAKEN..."

DOG

YOUR INCESSANT PAGE FLIPPING HAS COOLED MY PASTA. GO HEAT IT UP.

DOG CARE MANUAL

SLOW DOWN...RELAX...DON'T GULP YOUR FOOD FOR ONCE! YOU DO NOT LIVE IN A DOG PACK! THERE ARE NO OTHER DOGS HERE! NO ONE WANTS TO STEAL YOUR FOOD!

YOU ARE A DOMESTICATED HOUSE PET! THE URGE TO COMPETE FOR FOOD IS ANCIENT, HEREDITARY BAGGAGE! THERE IS NO REASON TO BEHAVE LIKE YOUR BOORISH, PRIMITIVE ANCESTORS!

HERE.

GULP!

ELECTRA

RATS. ANOTHER MEAL RUINED BY THE RELATIVES.

ELECTRA

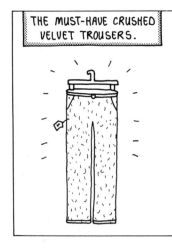

TONIGHT WE BEGIN YOUR EXERCISE PROGRAM WITH A BRISK ONE-MILE WALK, ELECTRA!

YAWN

I HAVE MY CASSETTE PLAYER, HEADPHONES, EXTRA TAPES, SQUIRT BOTTLE, ANKLE WEIGHTS, HAND WEIGHTS, AND MY WAIST-PACK CONTAINING MY KEYS, WALLET, MUGGER WHISTLE, SUNSCREEN, PEDOMETER, CONTACT CASE, CELLULAR PHONE, ORANGE SLICES, LIP BALM AND MUSCLE SPASM OINTMENT.

SPLAT.

Z Z Z Z Z Z

Guisewite

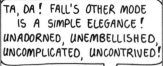

108

WE HAVEN'T HEARD FROM CATHY ALL WEEK. LET'S CALL AND SEE IF WE CAN WORM SOME INFORMATION OUT OF HER!

...NO! SHE WON'T TELL US ANYTHING! LET'S CALL HER FRIEND CHARLENE UNDER FALSE PRETENSES AND SEE IF WE CAN GET HER TO CRACK!

...NO! LET'S DRIVE TO CATHY'S HOUSE, PARK ACROSS THE STREET AND SEE IF WE CAN CATCH A VISUAL SIGHTING!

BUSYBODY: WORKOUT PROGRAM FOR MOTHERS.

I WEPT DURING "SLEEPLESS IN SEATTLE," AND CAN SPONTANEOUSLY QUOTE PASSAGES FROM "THE BRIDGES OF MADISON COUNTY" IN MOMENTS OF PASSION...

I CAN DISCUSS MARRIAGE WITHOUT RUNNING... CHILDREN WITHOUT CHOKING... FEELINGS WITHOUT GAGGING... AND YES! I NOTICED YOUR DARLING NEW BOOTS!

I HAVE STRENGTH, POWER, MONEY, WIT AND THE GRACE TO SENSE WHEN A PRETTY LADY JUST NEEDS A HUG!

WHICH OF US IS EVER REALLY PREPARED TO MEET THE MAN OF OUR DREAMS?

PLEASE SEAT THIS COUPLE.

WE'RE NOT A COUPLE.

WE'RE JUST FRIENDS.

WE'RE NOT REALLY EVEN FRIENDS.

WE'RE ACQUAINTANCES.

WE'RE TWO PEOPLE THROWN TOGETHER BY A MUTUAL NEED FOR FOOD AND HUMAN -- YET COMPLETELY PLATONIC -- CONTACT!

WE ARE NOT AND NEVER WILL BE ROMANTICALLY INVOLVED! WE ARE BOTH COMPLETELY AVAILABLE!

ONE CHECK, SEPARATE TABLES.

HERE'S MY BUSINESS CARD. DON'T BE SHY.

111

MOM! IRVING SHOWED UP AT THE RESTAURANT WHERE I'M HAVING DINNER WITH BRADLEY! WHAT SHOULD I DO??

SOAK STAINS IN LEMON JUICE AND LAY THEM IN THE SUN! FOLD CLOTHES WHILE THEY'RE STILL WARM TO REDUCE IRONING TIME!

EAT FRUIT IN THE MORNING! CLEAN THE TUB EACH TIME YOU USE IT! DO A GOOD DEED EVERY DAY, AND WHEN ALL ELSE FAILS, TRY VINEGAR!

UM...OK, MOM. THANKS.

ANOTHER MOTHER, PREPARED FOR HER DOCTORAL THESIS, SOMEHOW MANAGES TO FLUNK THE POP QUIZ.

....HE LEFT? IRVING LEFT??

PLEASANT FELLOW. HOW DO YOU KNOW HIM?

HE TALKED TO YOU FOR 20 MINUTES, AND YOU DON'T KNOW HOW I KNOW HIM??

HOW WOULD I KNOW HOW YOU KNOW HIM?

I WAS EATING DINNER WITH YOU... HE WALKED UP... I RAN HYSTERICALLY TO THE LADIES ROOM... WAS GONE FOR 20 MINUTES... AND THE SUBJECT OF HOW I KNOW HIM NEVER CAME UP??!

NO. HOW DO YOU KNOW HIM?

AND, FURTHERMORE, WHY WOULD I WANT TO??

COULD YOU TELL IF IRVING MISSED ME??

CAN'T ANSWER. I'M TOO JEALOUS.

BRADLEY, WE HAVE NO INTEREST IN EACH OTHER, REMEMBER?? WE HAVE A PACT-- JUST FRIENDS!

I WANT YOU TO LUST AFTER ME THE WAY YOU DO HIM.

WE'RE SUPPOSED TO OFFER EACH OTHER IMPARTIAL, UNEMOTIONALLY INVOLVED INSIGHT INTO THE OPPOSITE SEX!

YOUR EYES ARE LIKE WILD, DANCING FLAMES!

INSIGHT NUMBER ONE: STICK WITH WOMEN FRIENDS.

If I pay bills and balance my checkbook, I won't get to the grocery store...

If I go to the grocery store, I won't do the bills, the checkbook, or the laundry... If I do the laundry, I won't do the bills, checkbook, groceries, write letters, read the paper, answer calls or clean the house...

If I sink into a depressed stupor and do nothing, it will all still be here tomorrow, only there will be more of it.

Forget the quest for perfection. All I really want is to get to stop and start all over.

Hello??

Hi, sweetie.

Oh. Hi, mom.

Uh, oh. Bad time to call?

No, it's a fine time to call.

Everything ok?

Everything's fine.

Ok. I just wanted to say hi.

Ok.

Bye, then.

Bye.

Attention mothers: No matter how much they love you, when you call after 10:00pm, you will always be the wrong person.

In the day, when we don't care how we look, we haul 25-pound purses, stuffed with every possible beauty product.

At night, when we want to look gorgeous, we're supposed to carry puny evening bags that will only hold a miniature brush and one dinky lipstick.

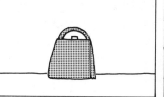

Life as a woman: One cruel joke after another.

I'll pay $100 for a tube of "barely there" concealer!

I'll go $150 for some dental floss!

Hairspray! Doesn't anyone have hairspray?!

RETURN PHONE CALLS.

...NO! FIRST FIND THE PAPERS THE CALLS ARE REGARDING AND THEN RETURN PHONE CALLS...
...NO! FIRST CLEAN OFF DESK, THEN FIND THE PAPERS, THEN RETURN PHONE CALLS...

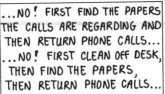

...NO! FIRST REORGANIZE FILE CABINETS TO MAKE ROOM, THEN CLEAN DESK, THEN FIND PAPERS, THEN RETURN CALLS...
...NO! FIRST ORDER LARGER FILE CABINETS, THEN REORGANIZE, THEN CLEAN, THEN FIND, THEN CALL.....

HELP!! I CAN'T GET MY BRAIN OUT OF REVERSE!!

7:00 AM: START THINKING ABOUT WHAT I'LL HAVE FOR DINNER.

10:00 AM: DREAM ABOUT MY DINNER.

12:00 PM: EAT LUNCH OBSESSING ABOUT DINNER.

3:00 PM: DWELL ON DINNER.

4:00 PM: LUST AFTER DINNER.

7:00 PM:

WHERE'S THE FOOD? THERE'S NO FOOD! THERE ISN'T ONE SCRAP OF FOOD HERE!!!

ONCE AGAIN I'VE SPENT THE DAY FANTASIZING, ONLY TO BE STOOD UP BY THE MAIN COURSE.

HELLO! HELLO! I'VE BEEN STANDING HERE FOR TEN MINUTES!

OH. DID YOU WANT SOMETHING?

RENTALS

WAIT A MINUTE! I WAS HERE FIRST!

OH. I DIDN'T SEE YOU.

1 HOUR CLEANING

SHE PUSHED HER CART RIGHT IN FRONT OF MINE!

OH. WERE YOU IN LINE?

CHECK OU

FORTUNATELY, I'M THE CENTER OF MY OWN UNIVERSE, AS I SEEM TO BE INVISIBLE TO EVERYONE ELSE.

117

119

I MADE A CALL TO HANDLE A PROBLEM. THE CALL GENERATED THREE OTHER CALLS.

THE OTHER CALLS GENERATED FOUR OTHER CALLS, AND NINE INDIVIDUAL PACKAGES OF PAPERWORK.

THE PACKAGES REQUIRED THE INVOLVEMENT OF SIX OTHER PEOPLE, ALL OF WHOM QUIT SPEAKING TO EACH OTHER AND ME DURING THE PROCESS, GENERATING A TOTAL OF FIFTEEN OTHER PROBLEMS.

I'VE REACHED THE POINT OF DIMINISHING RETURNS, AND IT'S ONLY 9:30 AM.

IN THE '50s, WOMEN STAYED HOME WITH THE CHILDREN.

I DON'T HAVE TO WORK!

IN THE '70s, WOMEN WENT OUT IN THE WORLD.

I WANT TO WORK!

TWENTY YEARS LATER... CONSCIOUSNESSES RAISED, VISIONS EXPANDED, DOORS OPENED, RESPECT RESTORED, CONFIDENCE BOOSTED, CHALLENGES MET... A WHOLE DYNAMIC, NEW BREED OF WOMEN FACE EACH OTHER AT THE PRE-SCHOOL DROP-OFF...

I DON'T HAVE TO WORK!

I'M TOO OLD FOR THIS.

THEY FOUND A HEMORRHOID CREAM THAT MADE WRINKLES DISAPPEAR...THEN A HIGH BLOOD PRESSURE MEDICINE THAT CURED BALDNESS...

THEN AN ACNE TREATMENT THAT REVERSED AGING...AND NOW THEY THINK THEY'RE ON-TO AN ASTHMA MEDICINE THAT MELTS FAT FROM THE THIGHS.

WHY DON'T I JUST GO TO THE DRUGSTORE, BUY ALL THE PRODUCTS, SMEAR THEM ON VARIOUS PARTS OF MY BODY AND SEE WHAT HAPPENS?!

SOME OF US CAN'T WAIT FOR SCIENCE.

Panel 1: I'LL PICK YOU UP AT 1:00, HONEY, AND THEN WE'LL GO ON A NATURE WALK WITH BRIANA AND HER MOM.

Pre-School

Panel 2: I'LL PICK YOU UP AT 1:00, SWEETHEART, AND THEN WE'LL GO TO YOUR CRAFT WORKSHOP WITH RYAN AND HIS MOM.

Pre-School

Panel 3: I'LL PICK YOU UP AT 5:30, ZENITH, AND THEN WE'LL RACE OVER, GET GUS FROM DAY CARE, GRAB DADDY AT HIS OFFICE, HURL TO THE CLEANERS, THE ATM, THE DRUG STORE AND THE GROCERY STORE, ZOOM HOME, DO THE BREAKFAST DISHES AND TRY TO WHIP TOGETHER SOME DINNER.

Panel 4: YOU HAVE TO STAY UNTIL 5:30?

I NEED THE REST.

Panel 5: BILLY'S MOM MADE A PAPIER-MÂCHÉ PILGRIM VILLAGE TO TEACH ZENITH'S CLASS ABOUT THANKSGIVING... I DIDN'T EVEN HAVE TIME TO BUY PAPER TOWELS LAST WEEK.

Panel 6: JENNIFER'S MOM DRESSED UP LIKE AN INDIAN AND DID A ONE-WOMAN SHOW ON HARVEST RITUALS FOR THE THREE-YEAR-OLDS... I COULDN'T EVEN FIND A CLEAN BLOUSE TO WEAR TO WORK.

Panel 7: OLIVIA'S MOM VOLUNTEERED TO MAKE PUMPKIN PIE FOR 37 FROM HER ORGANIC PUMPKIN PATCH... I CAN BARELY HEAT UP A FROZEN MEAL FOR FOUR.

Panel 8: I'M 40 YEARS OLD, AND I'M FLUNKING PRE-SCHOOL!

TWENTY YEARS IN BUSINESS, AND THE COMPETITION FINALLY GOT TO HER.

Panel 9: ALL THE OTHER MOTHERS BAKED COOKIES FOR ZENITH'S PRESCHOOL... SO, **TA DA! COOKIES!**

Panel 10: WHEN DID YOU HAVE TIME TO BAKE COOKIES?

I BOUGHT A BOX OF COOKIES, TORE OFF THE WRAPPER, THREW THEM IN THE OVEN AND BURNED THEM SO IT WOULD LOOK AS IF I MADE COOKIES.

Panel 11: I WANT EVERYONE TO KNOW THAT EVEN THOUGH I WORK, MY LITTLE ZENITH HAS SOMEONE WHO'S WILLING TO GO THAT EXTRA MILE FOR HER.

Panel 12: THE KEEBLER ELF.

RATS. I THOUGHT I'D SCRAPED ALL THOSE OFF.

MY MOTHER ISN'T GOING TO MAKE ME DETERIORATE THIS THANKSGIVING, ANDREA.

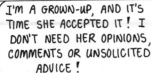

I'M A GROWN-UP, AND IT'S TIME SHE ACCEPTED IT! I DON'T NEED HER OPINIONS, COMMENTS OR UNSOLICITED ADVICE!

WITH EVERY BREATH I TAKE, MY ONLY THOUGHTS ARE FOR THE HAPPINESS OF MY CHILDREN.

WAAH! MOMMY!

EVERY TIME I'M AROUND A MOTHER, ANOTHER BABY GETS BORN.

MY NAILS HAVE BEEN DECENT. TODAY, I BIT THEM OFF... MY SKIN HAS BEEN FINE. TODAY, IT BROKE OUT.

MY DEMEANOR HAS BEEN POISED AND PROFESSIONAL. TODAY, I SPILLED COFFEE ON MY HAIR, RIPPED MY PANTY-HOSE, BROKE MY PURSE STRAP AND SAT ON THE FLOOR OF A 7-ELEVEN IN MY POWER SUIT AND ATE A BAG OF CHEETOS.

ANYTHING MOM WAS LIKELY TO PICK AT, I MADE WORSE. ANYTHING MOM WAS LIKELY TO CRITICIZE, I DESTROYED.

MOTHER'S LITTLE HELPER HAS COME HOME!

AND SHE'S BROUGHT HER FLEA-RIDDEN PUPPY.

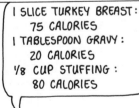

I SLICE TURKEY BREAST: 75 CALORIES
I TABLESPOON GRAVY: 20 CALORIES
1/8 CUP STUFFING: 80 CALORIES

1/8 CUP SWEET POTATOES: 45 CALORIES
1/4 INCH PUMPKIN PIE: 50 CALORIES
I DAB WHIPPED CREAM: 25 CALORIES

TOTAL MEAL: 295 CALORIES, 12 GRAMS OF FAT.

THE "PORTION CONTROL" APPROACH TO SENSIBLE HOLIDAY EATING: BEGUN, 4:15 PM ABANDONED, 4:17 PM.

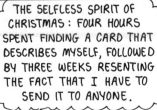

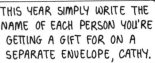